ZAGAT®

Best of
Toronto
2007/08

LOCAL EDITOR
Linda Barnard
STAFF EDITOR
Shelley Gallagher

Published and distributed by
Zagat Survey, LLC
4 Columbus Circle
New York, NY 10019
T: 212.977.6000
E: toronto@zagat.com
www.zagat.com

ACKNOWLEDGMENTS

We thank Gina Mallet, Steven Shukow, Alan A. Vernon and Nancy Wong, as well as the following members of our staff: Victoria Elmacioglu (associate editor) and Josh Rogers (assistant editor), Maryanne Bertollo, Sandy Cheng, Reni Chin, Larry Cohn, Jeff Freier, Caroline Hatchett, Roy Jacob, Natalie Lebert, Mike Liao, Dave Makulec, Andre Pilette, Becky Ruthenburg, Thomas Sheehan, Kilolo Strobert, Sharon Yates and Kyle Zolner.

Contents

About This Survey

This 2007/08 Best of Toronto Survey is an update reflecting significant developments since our last Survey was published. It covers 281 restaurants, bars and attractions, including 36 important additions, and indicates changes (e.g. new addresses, phone numbers) to existing properties. We've also included a selection of top-rated hotels.

WHO PARTICIPATED: Input from 1,719 surveyors forms the basis for the ratings and reviews in this guide (their comments are shown in quotation marks within the reviews). Collectively they bring roughly 203,000 annual meals worth of experience to this Survey. This guide is really "theirs."

OUR EDITOR: We are especially grateful to our local editor for this update, Linda Barnard, a freelance food writer and cocktail columnist for the *Toronto Star*.

ABOUT ZAGAT: This marks our 28th year reporting on the shared experiences of consumers like you. Today we have over 300,000 surveyors and now cover dining, entertaining, golf, hotels, movies, music, nightlife, resorts, shopping, spas, theatre and tourist attractions worldwide.

SHARE YOUR OPINION: We invite you to join any of our upcoming surveys – just register for free at **zagat.com,** where you can rate and review establishments year-round. Each participant will receive a complimentary copy of the resulting guide when published.

AVAILABILITY: Zagat guides are available in all major bookstores, by subscription at **zagat.com** and for use on mobile devices via **Zagat to Go.**

FEEDBACK: There is always room for improvement, thus we invite your comments and suggestions about any aspect of our performance. Just contact us at toronto@zagat.com.

New York, NY
June 29, 2007

Nina and Tim

Nina and Tim Zagat

What's New

Ontario's capital prides itself on its multicultural milieu, and the city's dining options – from haute to humble – reflect its global leanings. In fact, the restaurants in this Survey showcase nearly 35 cuisines. Given such culinary diversity, it's easy to understand why Torontonians report that they eat out an average of 2.7 meals per week.

DINING IN STYLE: With the tapas trend on the wane, chefs are now accommodating diners' desires for a square meal. Greg Couillard blasts into Bloor Yorkville with Spice Room & Chutney Bar, an exotic Eclectic. Midtown's Mirabelle offers Modern European fare. The comfort-food Canadian trevor kitchen & bar has opened up in the Downtown Core, while nearby Colborne Lane brings the talent of toque Claudio Aprile to a creative Eclectic menu.

KEEPING THE SPIRIT: A number of old favourites have shuttered, with new eateries eager to fill the void. The Danforth space that housed Belgian-French stalwart Café Brussel is now home to Globe Bistro, an Eclectic dabbling in molecular gastronomy. Those who've mourned the loss of Chris McDonald's Avalon welcome Cava, his new Spanish tapas and wine bar in Midtown. And though long-running jazz joint Montreal Bistro has closed its doors, the music plays on at Queen West West's Opal Jazz Lounge, offering French cuisine, and Bloor Yorkville's Sopra Upper Lounge, serving Italian fare.

BRIGHT LIGHTS, BIG CHANGES: Some veteran nightlife venues have revamped their images. The decade-old Fluid has reopened with dramatically updated decor, and after a brief closure, Courthouse Chamber Lounge near St. Lawrence Market has morphed into a swank live music spot called Live@Courthouse.

MUSEUM MAKEOVERS: Top architects are giving the city's attractions an update. Daniel Libeskind has designed a series of crystal-shaped additions for Bloor Yorkville's Royal Ontario Museum, while the Art Gallery of Ontario in Grange Park will soon get an elaborate redo courtesy of Toronto-born Frank Gehry.

Toronto   Linda Barnard
June 29, 2007

MOST POPULAR

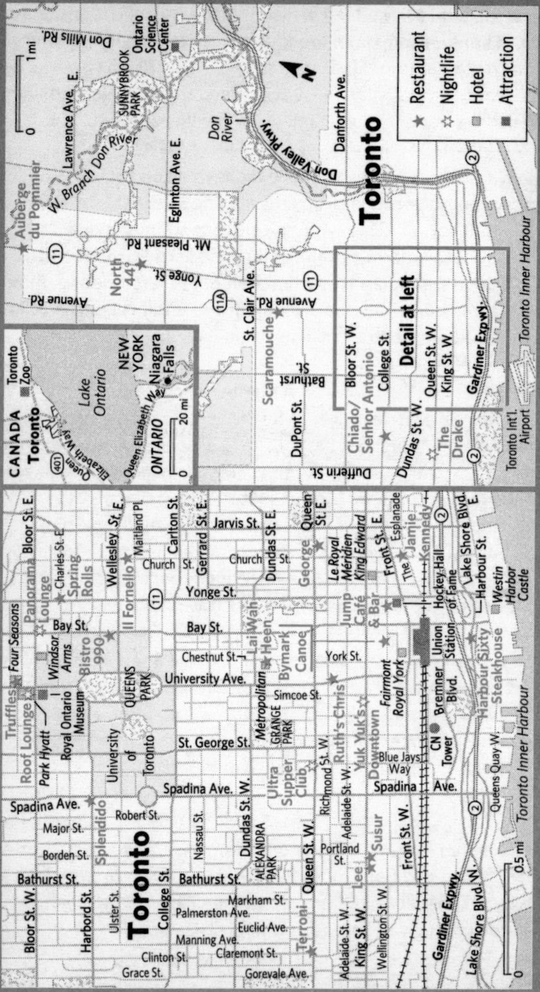

Map legend:
- ★ Restaurant
- ☆ Nightlife
- ⬡ Hotel
- ■ Attraction

Toronto

Detail at left

Toronto Inner Harbour

Inset map:
CANADA
Toronto
Lake Ontario
ONTARIO
NEW YORK
Niagara Falls
Queen Elizabeth Way
Toronto Zoo

Labels on main map:
Don Mills Rd.
Ontario Science Center
Lawrence Ave. E.
SUNNYBROOK PARK
W. Branch Don River
Eglinton Ave. E.
Don River
Danforth Ave.
Don Valley Pkwy.
Auberge du Pommier
Mt. Pleasant Rd.
North 44°
Yonge St.
St. Clair Ave.
Avenue Rd.
Scaramouche
Chiado / Senhor Antonio
Bloor St. W.
Queen St. W.
King St. W.
College St.
Bathurst St.
DuPont St.
Dundas St. W.
The Drake
Dufferin St.
Gardiner Expwy.
Toronto Int'l Airport
Toronto Inner Harbour

Detail / lower map labels:
Bloor St. E.
Panorama Bloor St. E.
Spring Rolls
Charles St.
Maitland Pl.
Wellesley St.
Carlton St.
Jarvis St.
Dundas St. E.
Queen St.
Esplanade
The Jamie
Il Fornello
Church
Gerrard St.
Church
George
Le Royal Meridien King Edward
Front St.
Lake Shore Blvd.
Truffles / Four Seasons
Windsor Arms
Lounge
Bay St.
Yonge St.
Bistro 990
JaiWah
Hockey Hall of Fame
Harbour St.
Roof Lounge
Park Hyatt
Chestnut St.
Heen
Bymark
Canoe
Lump Café & Bar
Union Station
Westin Harbour Castle
Royal Ontario Museum
University Ave.
York St.
Bremner Blvd.
Harbour Sixty Steakhouse
QUEENS PARK
Metropolitan GRANGE PARK
Simcoe St.
Ruth's Chris
Gairmont Royal York
University of Toronto
St. George St.
Yuk Yuk's
Downtown
CN Tower
Blue Jays Way
Spadina Ave.
Robert St.
Spadina Ave. W.
Ultra Supper Club
Richmond St. W.
Adelaide St. W.
Susur
Spadina Ave.
Queens Quay W.
Spadina Ave.
Major St.
Nassau St.
Dundas St. W.
ALEXANDRA PARK
Queen St. W.
Portland St.
Front St.
Borden St.
Bathurst St.
Bloor St. W.
Ulster St.
College St.
Bathurst St.
Markham St.
Palmerston Ave.
Adelaide St. W.
King St. W.
Wellington St. W.
Gardiner Expwy.
Lake Shore Blvd. W.
Harbord St.
Terroni
Euclid Ave.
Manning Ave.
Clinton St.
Claremont St.
Grace St.
Gorevale Ave.
Splendido
Toronto

6

Most Popular

Each surveyor has been asked to name his or her five favourite restaurants. This list reflects their choices.

1. Canoe
2. North 44°
3. Scaramouche
4. Susur
5. Jamie Kennedy
6. Bymark
7. Il Fornello
8. Auberge Pommier
9. Ruth's Chris Steak*
10. Truffles
11. Splendido
12. Harbour Sixty
13. Spring Rolls
14. Bistro 990
15. Terroni
16. George
17. Jump Café & Bar
18. Lee*
19. Chiado/Antonio
20. Lai Wah Heen

It's obvious that many of the above restaurants are among the Toronto area's most expensive, but if popularity were calibrated to price, we suspect that a number of other restaurants would join the above ranks. Given the fact that both our surveyors and readers love to discover dining bargains, we have added a list of 10 Best Buys on page 10.

The map on the facing page includes Toronto's Most Popular restaurants, nightspots and attractions, and some top hotels. See page 62 for a list of Most Popular nightlife venues, and page 70 for Most Popular attractions.

KEY NEWCOMERS

Following is our editors' take on some notable restaurant arrivals.

Cava
Colborne Lane
Globe Bistro
Jamie Kennedy/Gardiner
kaiseki-SAKURA
Kultura

Lai Toh Heen
Mirabelle
Opal Jazz
Spice Room & Chutney Bar
Torito
trevor kitchen & bar

---

* Indicates a tie with restaurant above

Ratings & Symbols

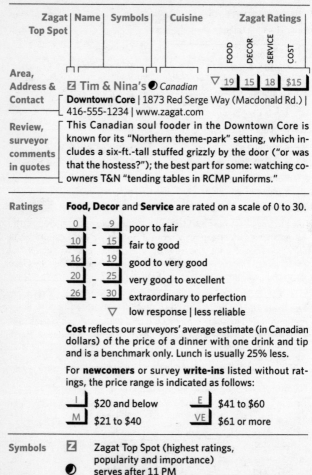

	Zagat Top Spot	Name	Symbols	Cuisine	Zagat Ratings			
					FOOD	DECOR	SERVICE	COST
Area, Address & Contact	☑ Tim & Nina's ◖ *Canadian*				▽ 19	15	18	$15
	Downtown Core	1873 Red Serge Way (Macdonald Rd.)	416-555-1234	www.zagat.com					
Review, surveyor comments in quotes	This Canadian soul fooder in the Downtown Core is known for its "Northern theme-park" setting, which includes a six-ft.-tall stuffed grizzly by the door ("or was that the hostess?"); the best part for some: watching co-owners T&N "tending tables in RCMP uniforms."							

Ratings

Food, Decor and **Service** are rated on a scale of 0 to 30.

0	– 9	poor to fair
10	– 15	fair to good
16	– 19	good to very good
20	– 25	very good to excellent
26	– 30	extraordinary to perfection
	▽	low response	less reliable

Cost reflects our surveyors' average estimate (in Canadian dollars) of the price of a dinner with one drink and tip and is a benchmark only. Lunch is usually 25% less.

For **newcomers** or survey **write-ins** listed without ratings, the price range is indicated as follows:

I	$20 and below		E	$41 to $60
M	$21 to $40		VE	$61 or more

Symbols

☑	Zagat Top Spot (highest ratings, popularity and importance)
◖	serves after 11 PM
ⓢ	closed on Sunday
Ⓜ	closed on Monday
⊘	no credit cards accepted

Top Food Ratings

Ratings are to the left of names. Lists exclude places with low votes.

29 Sushi Kaji

28 Scaramouche
Chiado/Antonio

27 North 44°
Hiro Sushi
Susur
Lai Wah Heen
Lee
Splendido
Oro
Bistro/Bakery Thuet
Perigee
Célestin
Scaramouche Pasta

26 George

Truffles
Canoe
Starfish Oyster
Boba
Opus
Il Mulino

25 Harbour Sixty
Mistura
Jamie Kennedy
Bymark
JOV
Mildred Pierce
Terra
Blowfish
Pangaea

BY CUISINE

CANADIAN

26 George
Canoe
25 Jamie Kennedy
24 Gallery Grill
20 Trapper's

CONTINENTAL

28 Scaramouche
27 North 44°
26 Opus
25 Bymark
Pangaea

ECLECTIC

25 Terra
Pangaea

24 Centro
Senses Bakery
Swan

FRENCH

27 Susur
Bistro/Bakery Thuet
Perigee
Célestin
26 Truffles

ITALIAN

27 Scaramouche Pasta
26 Il Mulino
25 Mistura
24 Tratt. Giancarlo
Zucca Trattoria

JAPANESE

29	Sushi Kaji
27	Hiro Sushi
25	Blowfish
24	Nami
	EDO

MEDITERRANEAN

27	Lee
	Splendido

Oro

Perigee

24	Auberge Pommier

SEAFOOD

28	Chiado/Antonio
26	Starfish Oyster
25	Penrose Fish & Chips
24	Rodney's Oyster
	Nami

Top Decor Ratings

26	Canoe		Gallery Grill
	Rain		North 44°
	Scaramouche		Sultan's Tent
	Truffles		Bymark
	Auberge Pommier		Scaramouche Pasta*
25	Lobby	24	Susur
	Courtyard Café		Ki

Top Service Ratings

27	Scaramouche		Splendido
	Scaramouche Pasta		Sushi Kaji
	Matignon		Jacques' Bistro
26	Truffles		Canoe
	Oro		Chiado/Antonio
25	North 44°		Lai Wah Heen
	Perigee		Auberge Pommier

Best Buys

In order of Bang for the Buck rating.

1.	Burrito Boyz	6.	Pho Hung
2.	Chippy's	7.	Bonjour Brioche
3.	Penrose Fish & Chips	8.	Fresh
4.	Salad King	9.	Izakaya
5.	Aunties & Uncles	10.	Swatow

RESTAURANTS
DIRECTORY

Restaurants

Toronto

Across The Road *Continental/Italian*
22 | 17 | 23 | $76

Midtown | 679 Mt. Pleasant Rd. (Eglinton Ave. E.) | 416-486-1111
Still "steady as she goes", this Continental–Northern Italian in Midtown "does all the basics well"; decorated in a colonial French style, the 46-seat room feels "cosy" and is populated with "friendly" staffers who help foster a "relaxed atmosphere."

Adega 🗷 *Portuguese/Seafood*
23 | 20 | 22 | $67

Downtown Core | 33 Elm St. (Yonge St.) | 416-977-4338 | www.adegarestaurante.ca
"I dig Adega" declare diners hooked on the "wonderful" seafood and "super" vintages at this "rustic", "casual" Portuguese just off Downtown's Yonge Street strip ("a nice choice for this area"); "client-oriented" servers who "know the menu and wine extremely well" also help provide "good value for the cost."

Allen's ◑ *Pub Food*
19 | 17 | 18 | $41

Danforth-Greektown | 143 Danforth Ave. (Broadview Ave.) | 416-463-3086 | www.allens.to
"Upmarket" Irish pub grub (e.g. "legendary sweet-potato fries" and "great" off-menu burgers) plus beer and scotch lists "to make an AA counselor cringe" and a "lovely garden" all add appeal to this "speakeasy-style" Danforth-Greektown veteran; "service can be spotty", however; N.B. no children after 8 PM.

Amuse-Bouche 🗷Ⓜ *French*
23 | 20 | 21 | $78

King West | 96 Tecumseth St. (King St. W.) | 416-913-5830 | www.amusebboucherestaurant.com
This "unpretentious" venue "hidden down a residential street" in King West amuses plenty of local *bouches* with its "excellent", "flavourful" New French fare ("delicious" tasting menus are "recommended", even if portions are "small"); "polished, gracious" servers are "friendly" too, so though the 30-seat dining room may be "cramped", most find the experience "well worth the crowding": you feel like "you're having an intimate dinner with everyone."

Annona *Eclectic*

20 | 20 | 22 | $70

Bloor Yorkville | Park Hyatt Hotel | 4 Avenue Rd. (Bloor St. W.) | 416-324-1567 | www.parktoronto.hyatt.com

Even the annona-mous are "treated like VIPs" at this Eclectic in Bloor Yorkville's Park Hyatt, courtesy of "efficient" staffers who proffer "complex" seasonal cuisine "prepared with delicacy" and paired with an extensive selection of wines; suits say the "upscale" room's sufficiently "subdued for business discussions", while couples deem the "dim" corners "romantic."

Asian Legend ● *Chinese*

19 | 18 | 14 | $30

Bayview Village | Finch & Leslie Plaza | 125 Ravel Rd. (Leslie St.) | 416-756-9388
Chinatown-Kensington | 418 Dundas St. W. (Parliament St.) | 416-977-3909
Thornhill | 505 Hwy. 7 E. (W. Beaver Creek Rd.) | 905-763-8211
York Mills | 5188 Yonge St. (Park Home Ave.) | 416-221-9797
www.asianlegend.ca

"Dumpling goodness", "authentic" entrees and comparatively "posh" dining rooms satisfy fans of this "reasonably priced" Chinese quartet, though critics who cite "inconsistent" quality and "lax" service consider these Sino sibs somewhat less than legendary.

☑ Auberge du Pommier ☒ *French/Mediterranean*

24 | 26 | 25 | $84

York Mills | Yonge Corporate Ctr. | 4150 Yonge St. (bet. Hwy. 401 & York Mills Rd.) | 416-222-2220 | www.aubergedupommier.com

Though it may be "odd" to see this "gloriously" "quaint" York Mills "gem" set "in the parking lot of a corporate high-rise", unfazed *amis* adore its "superb" New French–Med cuisine and "ever-improving wine list" served up by a "terrific" staff; it's "first-class" "for a business lunch" or special occasion ("ask for a table by the fireplace" if you "want her to fall in love with you"), but "you pay for it."

Aunties & Uncles Ⓜ⊟ *Diner*

22 | 14 | 16 | $21

South Annex | 74 Lippincott St. (College St.) | 416-324-1375

"Ample", "mouth-watering" brunches draw an "arty", "young" crowd to this South Annex diner, a "tiny" and "charmingly ramshackle" haunt outfitted with "kitschy mismatched furniture" (even the tables on the patio are "off-kilter"); though surveyors are split on service ("quick" vs. "inefficient"), all advise "arrive early" on weekends to avoid "long line-ups"; N.B. kitchen closes at 3 PM.

Avant Goût *French*

| - | - | - | E |

Rosedale-Summerhill | 1108 Yonge St. (Roxborough St.) | 416-916-3681

Recently relocated to Yonge Street, this warm, intimate Rosedale restaurant will have you thinking you're in Paris as you sample chef-owner Kamal Hani's Moroccan-inflected French cuisine; an extensive wine list and elegant environs – think dark-wood panelling and sparkling chandeliers – contribute to the romantic vibe.

Avenue ● *Eclectic*

| 22 | 22 | 22 | $64 |

Bloor Yorkville | Four Seasons | 21 Avenue Rd. (Yorkville Ave.) | 416-928-7332 | www.fourseasons.com/toronto

A "superb Sunday brunch" is the standout at this contemporary lounge in Bloor Yorkville's Four Seasons hotel, but the venue's "suitable for all purposes" ("a first date, business meeting or dinner with family and friends") thanks to "reliably" "refined" Eclectic fare, a "great floor staff" and a bar scene that's "more mature than the usual" – if a bit "expensive" ("the best $18 martini I've ever had"), not surprising in this ritzy neighbourhood.

Babur *Indian*

| 22 | 16 | 17 | $31 |

Queen West | 273 Queen St. W. (McCaul St.) | 416-599-7720 | www.babur.ca

Set in a "key" Queen West location with "large glass windows" for "great people-watching", this "clean, semicasual" Indian delivers with a "hard-to-beat" buffet at lunchtime and "traditional" fare for dinner; though some would like it hotter ("the spice is toned down for Saturday shoppers"), most find the eats an "excellent value", so "be prepared to wait for a table."

NEW Balsam Ⓜ *Italian*

| - | - | - | M |

The Beach | 2343 Queen St. E. (Balsam Ave.) | 416-699-2343

Toronto's unique Beach district has a fresh new face with the opening of this Italian restaurant that's taken over the former Peppino's on the Beach space, offering both small plates (fresh pappardelle with white truffle cream sauce) in addition to more substantial entrees; there's a small, pleasant dining room, but nature-lovers may prefer sitting in one of the two pretty outdoor gardens.

	FOOD	DECOR	SERVICE	COST

bar_one *Italian/Pizza*　　　　　19 | 20 | 19 | $45

Queen West Gallery District | 924 Queen St. W. (Shaw St.) | 416-535-1655 | www.bar-one.com

Owned by the Barone family (get it?), this modern, "minimal" and marble-accented Italian in the Queen West Gallery District is known for "crispy", "delicious" thin-crust pizza, but admirers aver it also boasts a "terrific" brunch served by an "above-average" staff; others feel that given the "cool crowd", it's "better as a bar than a restaurant"; N.B. it now serves lunch.

Barberian's Steak House ● *Steak*　　23 | - | 23 | $76

Downtown Core | 7 Elm St. (Yonge St.) | 416-597-0335 | www.barberians.com

This "landmark" steakhouse in the Downtown Core is a "paradise" for "vintage lovers" thanks to a "superb" vino list "the size of a phone book" to go with the menu's "juicy" chops; whether you're there "for business or pleasure", the "attentive" owners and staff will make you "feel at ease"; N.B. a recent redo expanded the dining room and added a two-story, underground wine cellar.

Batifole *French*　　　　　▽ 25 | 15 | 21 | $73

Riverdale | 744 Gerrard St. E. (bet. Broadview & Carlaw Aves.) | 416-462-9965

Without question the "best French in [Riverdale's] Chinatown East", this "hidden jewel" has respondents raving *"la vraie de vraie"*; Francophiles laud "excellent", "authentic" Gallic cuisine, a *terroir*-specific wine list and "knowledgeable staffers" (all of which keep the place "true to its roots"); a "classic" room with an "unpretentious" vibe completes the package; N.B. closed Tuesdays.

beerbistro ● *French*　　　　18 | 18 | 18 | $48

Financial District | 18 King St. E. (Victoria St.) | 416-861-9872 | www.beerbistro.com

"Bring your liver" and your sense of adventure to this Financial District French bistro that "incorporates beer into many dishes" in an "upscale twist on the pub theme" (the kitchen even serves till 1 AM); offering "friendly service", "modern" decor and, of course, an "outstanding selection" of suds, it's "popular" with the "business crowd"; N.B. it now offers Sunday brunch.

| | FOOD | DECOR | SERVICE | COST |

Bellini's *Italian* — 21 | 18 | 21 | $61

Bloor Yorkville | 101 Yorkville Ave. (bet. Avenue Rd. & Bay St.) |
416-929-9111 | www.bellinisristorante.com

A "below-ground-level" "hideaway" with "upscale" food, this Northern
Italian in "trendy" Bloor Yorkville remains a "classic" "special-
occasion" spot ("take your valentine"); "polished" servers who handle
you "with care" and a "restful", "romantic" ambience add to the "old-
school fine-dining" experience enjoyed by "celebs, gourmands" and
"visitors from overseas."

Biagio Ristorante 🅢 *Italian* — 20 | 18 | 22 | $72

St. Lawrence | 155 King St. E. (Jarvis St.) | 416-366-4040
Ensconced in historic St. Lawrence Hall, this spacious, "elegant"
Northern Italian staffed by "informed", "hospitable folks" proffers
"delightful", "dependable" fare and an "excellent" 1,500-label wine
list; meanwhile, daters declare summer dining "by the fountain" on
the "beautiful patio" "could not be more romantic."

Biff's Bistro & Wine Bar 🅢 *French* — 21 | 21 | 22 | $72

St. Lawrence | 4 Front St. E. (Yonge St.) | 416-860-0086 |
www.oliverbonacini.com

Fans of this "straightforward French bistro" ("well-executed" entrees,
"excellent-value" prix fixe meals, "amazing cheeses") find the "nicely
appointed" Parisian-style venue in St. Lawrence "convenient for a pre-
show dinner" – not least because "intelligent" servers know how to accommodate theatregoers just before curtain time, when "everyone
wants to get their bills at once"; N.B. a post-Survey chef change may
outdate the above Food score.

🆉 Bistro & Bakery Thuet 🅼 *French* — 27 | 23 | 23 | $100

King West | 609 King St. W. (Bathurst St.) | 416-603-2777 |
www.thuet.ca

"Outstanding and original culinary delights" await at this Alsatian bistro in King West where "daring" chef-owner Marc Thuet dreams up
"seasonal", loftily priced dishes to be paired with "aspirational" wines
from an "extensive" list; diners can "focus on the flavour" thanks to an
unobtrusively "comfortable" dining room and the "discreet" atten-
tions of a "right-on" staff; N.B. they've recently added a glassed-in
bakery area as well as a 35-seat private room beneath the kitchen.

RESTAURANTS

	FOOD	DECOR	SERVICE	COST

☒ Bistro 990 *French/Mediterranean* — 23 | 21 | 22 | $69

Downtown Core | 990 Bay St. (Wellesley St.) | 416-921-9990 |
www.bistro990.ca

"Still full of the beautiful people" – including "Hollywood types" "during the International Film Festival" – this "charming" French-Med in the Downtown Core augments its "see-and-be-seen" reputation with "delectable" fare, a "warm, inviting and lively" atmosphere and "hardworking", "attentive" servers; a vocal minority opines it's "overrated" and "overpriced" and cautions "the staff knows if you're a somebody or a nobody – hopefully you're a somebody."

Bloom ☒Ⓜ *Continental* — ▽ 24 | 22 | 24 | $77

Bloor West Village | 2315 Bloor St. W. (bet. Durie St. & Windermere Ave.) |
416-767-1315 | www.bloomrestaurant.com

Garnering garlands for its "excellent" fusion-tinged fare and "well-executed" service, this "consistent" Continental in Bloor West Village is dubbed a "great repeat place"; minimalist, neutral-toned decor lends the 36-seat space a "hip vibe", in contrast to the theme pubs and old-country delis nearby; N.B. be aware that BYO is permitted.

Blowfish ☒ *Japanese* — 25 | 24 | 19 | $75

King West | 668 King St. W. (Bathurst St.) | 416-860-0606 |
www.blowfishrestaurant.com

"Hot crowd, cool food" is the line on this "trendy" French-influenced Japanese in King West, where "thirtysomethings" savor "outstanding", "inventive" entrees and sushi; housed in a former bank, the "stylish" eatery "pulsates" on weekends thanks to an on-site DJ – the "reverberations" may explain why servers are sometimes "inattentive" – so though the experience is "expensive", most find the "empty wallet" "worth it."

Boba ☒ *American* — 26 | 21 | 24 | $79

Bloor Yorkville | 90 Avenue Rd. (bet. Bloor St. & Davenport Rd.) |
416-961-2622 | www.boba.ca

This "high-end" Bloor Yorkville veteran remains "a favourite year after year" due to its "exquisite", "savoury" New American cuisine and the "gems" on the "well-selected wine list"; the husband-and-wife chef-owners are "consummate hosts" to boot, so most folks don't mind the "small" confines inside the "elegant" Victorian-era manse: just "hope your neighbours are interesting conversationalists."

	FOOD	DECOR	SERVICE	COST

Bodega *French*
22 | 17 | 19 | $56

Grange Park | 30 Baldwin St. (McCaul St.) | 416-977-1287 |
www.bodegarestaurant.com

"The classiest place on Baldwin Street", this Grange Park bistro pleases its "regular clientele" with "guaranteed-quality" Gallic goodies in "generous portions", served by "accommodating" staffers; the "little boîte" is decorated in an "upscale" French Provençal style and features a working fireplace; N.B. they've recently added a bar area.

Bonjour Brioche Ⓜ 🍴 *French*
23 | 15 | 16 | $22

Leslieville | 812 Queen St. E. (Broadview Ave.) | 416-406-1250

"Memorably" "delicious" fresh-baked quiches, tarts and croissants make this "cheery" cafe/patisserie seem like "a slice of France" in Leslieville; ok, the "tiny" room is unquestionably "cramped" ("go early or late to avoid the weekend brunch line-up"), but the "tantalizing" pastries and the "wonderfully smarmy" staff are said to be "well worth the elbow fights"; N.B. closed Mondays and Tuesdays.

Boujadi Ⓜ *Moroccan*
23 | 18 | 20 | $35

Forest Hill | 999 Eglinton Ave. W. (Old Park Rd.) | 416-440-0258 |
www.boujadi.com

Diners looking for "something different" dig the "African–Middle Eastern flair" of this "comfortable" Forest Hill Moroccan where "nicely prepared tagines and couscous dishes" are doled out in "generous portions"; "friendly" servers help create a "casual" vibe at this "great neighbourhood place" that's "worth the drive."

Boulevard Café *Peruvian*
21 | 16 | 17 | $40

South Annex | 161 Harbord St. (Borden St.) | 416-961-7676

"Fish and meat grilled to perfection" bring boulevardiers into this "cosy" South Annex Peruvian where the dining room may be "more shabby than chic" but comes with a "lovely patio" to compensate; servers are "personable" too, though critics caution you may need to use "active attention-getting techniques" to summon them.

Brassaii ◑ *American*
20 | 24 | 19 | $60

King West | 461 King St. W. (Spadina Ave.) | 416-598-4730 |
www.brassaii.com

"Young professionals and businesspeople" flock to this "cool" "refurbished" warehouse in King West to sup on "tasty" New American eats backed by an "excellent wine list"; proponents praise the "gorgeous" loftlike room furnished in muted greys and populated by "accommodating" staffers, but critics consider the setting "sparse" and say "service leaves much to be desired."

Brownes Bistro *Eclectic*   19 | 15 | 19 | $63

Rosedale-Summerhill | 4 Woodlawn Ave. E. (Yonge St.) | 416-924-8132

"Dependable" Eclectic eats make this Rosedale-Summerhill veteran a "standby" for area "families, couples and between-wifers" who also like the "comfort" of the bistro-style surroundings; however, a vocal minority scolds "snooty" staffers who sometimes dispel the "pleasant" vibe of this "neighbourhood spot."

Burrito Boyz *Mexican*   23 | 6 | 17 | $10

Entertainment District | 120 Peter St. (Richmond St. W.) | 416-593-9191
Entertainment District | 218 Adelaide St. W. (Duncan St.) | 647-439-4065 🗷
www.burritoboyz.ca

"It's not about the decor", it's about value at these Entertainment District Mexican "take-out joints" that deliver the city's Best Bang for the Buck; the "enormous custom-made burritos" sold "dirt-cheap" ("splurge for the homemade guac") have achieved "cult status", as evidenced by the midday and late-night weekend crowds that willingly wait in "line-ups out the door" – even in the "cold Toronto winter."

🛿 Bymark 🗷 *Continental*   25 | 25 | 23 | $98

Financial District | 66 Wellington St. W. (bet. Bay & York Sts.) | 416-777-1144 | www.bymarkdowntown.com

This "subterranean Valhalla" in the Financial District is frequented by "brokers and bankers" bullish on Mark McEwen's "innovative" Continental cookery; whether in the minimalist, "soothing" (if "dark") dining room, the "intimate" lounge or out on the warm-weather patio, an "efficient" crew provides "personalized service"; and if "outrageous" tabs have some figuring this spot's "reputation exceeds its price/value quotient", plenty more deem it "worth every cent."

Byzantium *Continental*   19 | 21 | 20 | $48

Church & Wellesley | 499 Church St. (Wellesley St.) | 416-922-3859
Revered by regulars as the "best gay restaurant in the gay village", this "stylish" Church and Wellesley Continental with a "European cafe

feel" offers "excellent-value" midweek prix fixe dinners plus "eye candy" (including "cute", "funny servers"); on weekends, DJs pump up the jam to bolster a "loud" bar scene.

Cajú 🗷 🖩 Brazilian — | — | — | M

Queen West Gallery District | 922 Queen St. W. (Shaw St.) | 416-532-2550 | www.caju.ca

Named after the tropical cashew fruit, this Brazilian in the Queen West Gallery District focuses on meat-, bean- and seafood-filled stews and other Amazonian specialties as a counterpoint to its sleek, modern decor; bossa nova on the stereo and specialty caipirinhas at the bar underscore that this place is the Rio thing.

⛵ Canoe 🗷 Canadian 26 | 26 | 25 | $88

Financial District | Toronto Dominion Bank Tower | 66 Wellington St. W., 54th fl. (Bay St.) | 416-364-0054 | www.canoerestaurant.com

Voted the city's No. 1 for both Decor and Popularity, this literally "top-tier" "destination" on the 54th floor of the Toronto Dominion Bank Tower lives up to its "stunning location" with "exquisitely flavoured" Canadian cuisine that's "presented with class" by a "first-rate" staff; prices that are "as lofty as the setting" don't deter those devotees who say the view alone justifies "the cost of your meal"; P.S. it's "worth waiting or bribing" to snag the large table "in the southwest corner, overlooking [the skyline] and lake."

Casa Barcelona! Spanish 21 | 15 | 19 | $57

Islington-Kingsway | 2980 Bloor St. W. (Royal York Rd.) | 416-234-5858 | www.casabarcelona.ca

It's "cheaper than a trip to Spain" – and quicker too: a "great night out" at this "cosy" Islington-Kingsway Iberian involves a "huge menu" of "authentic" eats ("delicious tapas"), an "unrivaled and well-priced" wine cellar and live flamenco and guitar shows; ok, the "decor could use some refreshing" ("lots of bullfight paintings"), but "witty, hospitable" owners lend the place a "welcoming" air.

NEW Cava Spanish — | — | — | E

Midtown | 1560 Yonge St. (Heath St.) | 416-979-9918 | www.cavarestaurant.ca

Veteran chef-owner Chris McDonald (of the now-shuttered Avalon) shows off his range at this Midtown tapas and wine bar that offers traditional Spanish treats as well as dishes delivering French, Italian and Mexican flair, from sardines done two ways to chipotle-caramel popcorn; the Basque-centric wine selection is as extensive as the food menu, and it's all served up in a simple, rustic setting.

☑ Célestin ☒Ⓜ French

27 | 22 | 22 | $86

Midtown | 623 Mt. Pleasant Rd. (Manor Rd. E.) | 416-544-9035
Best "savoured one plate at a time", chef-owner Pascal Ribreau's "refined", "creative" New French cuisine makes this Midtown "haute bistro" one of "the top spots in town"; "everything is above par here", including "knowledgeable" personnel and a renovated 1920s bank building interior that's "upscale", "clean" and "calm"; P.S. fans of the "to-die-for handmade bread" can stop by the "exquisite bakery next door" and get some to go.

Centro Restaurant & Lounge ☒ Eclectic

24 | 23 | 23 | $84

North Toronto | 2472 Yonge St. (Eglinton Ave.) | 416-483-2211 | www.centro.ca
The city's "who's who" still "schmooze, booze" and "people-watch" at this "chic" North Toronto "class act", recently refreshed via a $1.5 million face-lift; Bruce Woods' "sophisticated" Eclectic fare "lives up to its great reputation", as does the "incredible" 700-label wine cellar, and though a few bemoan "snobby" service, most say staffers "go the extra mile."

Cfood Ⓜ Seafood

– | – | – | E

Midtown | 2419 Yonge St. (bet. Broadway & Roselawn Aves.) | 416-544-1661 | www.cfood.com
Living up to its cheeky name with funky nautical decor, this self-styled 'concept restaurant' in Midtown offers a variety of market-fresh seafood that's grilled, baked or beer-battered to order as well as inventive starters and sides; there's even a bowl on each table containing a live Japanese fighting fish – which can be yours for a small donation that goes to the North York General Hospital.

☑ Chiado/Senhor Antonio Portuguese/Seafood

28 | 21 | 25 | $80

Little Italy | 864 College St. (Concord Ave.) | 416-538-1910 | www.chiadorestaurant.com
"Melt-in-your-mouth" seafood lures pescavores to this "top-notch" **Little Italy Portuguese** where "simple preparations emphasize" "su-

"perb" ingredients and the cellar contains what may be the "best Portuguese wine list in Canada"; staffers work so smoothly as to be "almost invisible" within the "intimate" old-world dining room and the minimalist tapas bar next door; yes, tabs are "steep" – but then "you've got to be terrific to charge these prices in this part of town."

Chippy's ⊘ British

| 23 | 11 | 17 | $15 |

Annex | 490 Bloor St. W. (bet. Albany & Howland Aves.) | 416-516-7776
Queen West | 893 Queen St. W. (Gorvale Ave.) | 416-866-7474 | www.chippys.ca

Chipper cognoscenti chirp "you can almost taste the Thames in every bite" of the "authentic, delicious" fried halibut, seafood cakes and chips served at these "retro", diner-style British "holes in the wall" in the Annex and Queen West; "efficient" staffers "batter and cook your order in full view" to "hip music", but the spots offer "minimal seating."

NEW Coca ◐ Spanish

| – | – | – | E |

Queen West West | 783 Queen St. W. (Claremont St.) | 416-703-0783

The newest venture from the owner of nearby Czehoski, this cosy Queen West West addition is a foodie's delight, featuring chef Nathan Isberg's upscale, inventive Spanish tapas (including the namesake Catalan pizza) on the main floor, more substantial meals and a full bar on the second level and private dining in the loft area above; a decent wine list and a hip earth-toned setting add to the experience.

NEW Colborne Lane ◐⊠Ⓜ Eclectic

| – | – | – | VE |

Downtown Core | 45 Colborne St. (Leader Ln.) | 416-368-9009 | www.colbornelane.com

At this edgy Downtown Core eatery, chef-owner Claudio Aprile (ex Senses) whips up sophisticated, pricey Eclectic creations that won't be pigeonholed – think Peking duck with licorice sauce – plus a $149 15-course tasting menu that truly displays the toque's range; it's all set in a historic building amid modern decor and rock 'n' roll background music; N.B. open Tuesday–Saturday for dinner only.

College Street Bar ◐ Italian

| 19 | 17 | 19 | $37 |

Little Italy | 574 College St. (Clinton St.) | 416-533-2417 | www.collegestreetbar.com

"Fun, funky and easy" is how fans describe this "unpretentious" Little Italy trattoria where the "cool bar food" includes pastas and risotto and the "service comes with a smile"; add in a garden patio, nightly live music, a long martini list and microbrewed beers, and the result is a "nice place to chill"; N.B. open till 2 AM.

Coppi Ristorante 🅫 *Italian* | 21 | 17 | 19 | $67 |

North Toronto | 3363 Yonge St. (bet. Golfdale Rd. & Snowdon Ave.) | 416-484-4464 | www.coppiristorante.com

Coppi cats consider this "comfortable" North Toronto Italian a "find", praising "well-made" *cucina* (e.g. "spectacular" risotto) and a "varied" selection of wines from The Boot, all brought to table by an "attentive" crew; the place is named in honour of famed cyclist Fausto Coppi, so expect to "eat surrounded by pictures" of him.

Corner House 🅫🅜 *European* | 24 | 20 | 22 | $68 |

Annex | 501 Davenport Rd. (Spadina Ave.) | 416-923-2604 | www.cornerhouserestaurant.com

"One of the most romantic spots in the city", this "charming", "discreet" converted house "hidden away close to the Casa Loma" features chef/co-owner Herbert Barnsteiner's "delicious" and "technically superb" Modern European cuisine; "warm" service and a patio also help to make it "perfect for a meet-the-parents dinner."

Courtyard Café *Eclectic* | - | 25 | 21 | $76 |

Bloor Yorkville | Windsor Arms Hotel | 18 St. Thomas St. (Bloor St. W.) | 416-921-2921 | www.windsorarmshotel.com

"An oasis of calm" in bustling Bloor Yorkville, this Eclectic in the Windsor Arms Hotel boasts a "cathedral-ceilinged dining room" with "fresh flowers" that's a "favourite" of "glitter girls and ladies who lunch"; proponents praise "fancy" fare that's "beautifully presented", while critics sigh over "friendly" yet "inattentive" servers.

Crush Wine Bar 🅫 *French/Mediterranean* | 22 | 22 | 22 | $67 |

King West | 455 King St. W. (Spadina Ave.) | 416-977-1234 | www.crushwinebar.com

Oenophiles "have a crush" on this King West bistro where a "massive wine list" (featuring "great by-the-glass options") is matched with "light, fresh and quite tasty" "classic" French-Med fare; staffed by a "good-looking", "friendly" crew, the "bustling" boîte attracts a "fun mix of designers, investment bankers and occasional celebrities", although a few noise-haters nix the "loud", loft-style setting.

NEW Cucina ●Ⓜ *Italian*

FOOD	DECOR	SERVICE	COST
–	–	–	M

Little Italy | 640 College St. (Grace St.) | 416-532-3841

Don't be fooled by the simple menu at this Southern Italian eatery on College Street, as the rustic fare – hand-cut pastas as well as pizzas and panini – is both fresh and seasonal; a casual atmosphere complete with a patio for people-watching draws a twentysomething crowd, especially in summer, when the kitchen is open seven days a week until 2 AM; N.B. plans are in the works for a second location.

Cuisine of India *Indian*

FOOD	DECOR	SERVICE	COST
22	11	16	$36

Willowdale | 5222 Yonge St. (bet. Finch & Sheppard Aves.) | 416-229-0377

"Tasty, fresh" eats make this "unprepossessing" Willowdale Indian a "good choice"; served by "friendly", "brisk" staffers, a meal here can be an "excellent value", even if the "shabby" room does look to some "like a suburban wallpaper store."

Czehoski ● *French/Italian*

FOOD	DECOR	SERVICE	COST
19	24	18	$71

Queen West West | 678 Queen St. W. (bet. Bathurst St. & Palmerston Ave.) | 416-366-6787 | www.czehoski.com

"Creative across the board" is the consensus on this Queen West West "former Czech butcher shop", now a "cutting-edge" eatery with contemporary wood-and-steel decor; boosters back the kitchen's "daring" New French–Italian preparations, but detractors deride the fare as "too precious" and say the service "isn't the best" either; P.S. wallet-watchers find it "better (and cheaper)" to sup in one of the "great bar areas" or on the rooftop garden patio.

Didier ⓈⓂ *French*

FOOD	DECOR	SERVICE	COST
▽ 22	19	18	$91

Midtown | 1496 Yonge St. (St. Clair Ave. W.) | 416-925-8588 | www.restaurantdidier.com

For traditional, "timeless" Gallic standards and "very good French and Canadian wines", Didier Leroy's "warm and inviting", old-world-style Midtowner "is the real thing"; staffed by "friendly" personnel, it's an "upscale" venue "with prices to match."

NEW Doku 15 *Japanese*

FOOD	DECOR	SERVICE	COST
–	–	–	E

Downtown Core | Cosmopolitan Hotel & Spa | 8 Colborne St. (Yonge St.) | 416-368-3658 | www.doku15.com

Although the name translates to 'poison', the Japanese cuisine at this restaurant in the Downtown Core's Cosmopolitan Hotel & Spa is any-

	FOOD	DECOR	SERVICE	COST

thing but: one half of the menu focuses on sushi, sashimi and rolls, while the other section showcases dumplings, entrees and creative small plates; all of the fare is made using quality ingredients and is prepared with flair, and the venue also boasts an adjoining bar serving a variety of sake-based cocktails.

Dragon Dynasty ⊠ *Chinese*

20 | **14** | **16** | **$32**

Scarborough | Chartwell Shopping Ctr. | 2301 Brimley Rd. (south of Finch Rd.) | 416-321-9000

There's little foot-draggin' when "locals" line up for the "awesome dim sum" and "traditional" dinner entrees at this Mandarin set in a Scarborough shopping centre; decorated Hong Kong–style, the expansive, "lively" place is popular for wedding parties and "frequent banquets", so "be prepared to wait."

EAST! Asian Street Fair *Pan-Asian*

17 | **22** | **18** | **$29**

Queen West | 240 Queen St. W. (John St.) | 416-351-3278

"Foods of the East" come to Queen West at this "lively" Pan-Asian sister to Spring Rolls that's known for its "cool", modern decor; staffers "efficiently" serve up the "interesting" if "not totally authentic" eats (all-day "dim sum is a nice touch") to "funky types" who wash it all down with "strong", "cheap martinis."

EDO Ⓜ *Japanese*

24 | **18** | **20** | **$52**

Forest Hill | 484 Eglinton Ave. W. (1½ blocks north of Avenue Rd.) | 416-322-3033 | www.edosushi.com

At this dimly lit Forest Hill Japanese, chef Ryo Ozawa whips up a "wonderful variety" of "innovative" sushi and "out-of-this-world" omakase – plus "truly amazing Kobe beef burgers"; a "friendly" staff helps foster a "warm, inviting" vibe, so though wallet-watchers warn eating here can be "expensive", "locals love it."

EDO-ko *Japanese/Seafood*

23 | **15** | **20** | **$46**

Forest Hill | 431 Spadina Rd. (north of St. Clair Ave. W.) | 416-482-8973 | www.edosushi.com

Aficionados laud "consistently fresh" sushi and "excellent" Japanese seafood whipped up by "sociable chefs" at this "casual" Forest Hill venue, younger brother to the nearby EDO; meanwhile, the "small" space elicits mixed reviews ("cosy" vs. "cramped"); N.B. unlike its sibling, this spot serves lunch.

	FOOD	DECOR	SERVICE	COST

Edward Levesque's Kitchen ⓜ *American* — — — | M

Leslieville | 1290 Queen St. E. (bet. Alton & Hastings Aves.) | 416-465-3600 | www.edwardlevesque.ca

Chef-owner Edward Levesque has transformed a former greasy spoon in Leslieville into this serious yet casual New American eatery where the emphasis is on fresh, seasonal food (much of it from organic farms) plus housemade desserts; the simple space is highlighted by long banquettes and an open kitchen, and in-the-know locals are already lining up for the weekend brunch.

Epic *French* | 24 | 23 | 23 | $75

Financial District | Fairmont Royal York Hotel | 100 Front St. W. (bet. Bay & York Sts.) | 416-860-6949 | www.fairmont.com

Epicures enthuse about the "mouth-watering", "innovative" cuisine and 800 wines on offer at this "unusually good" "high-end" French in the Financial District's Fairmont Royal York Hotel; though the "comfortably" upholstered dining room seats 150, surveyors say it has a "surprisingly intimate" feel, fostered by a staff that provides "timely yet unhurried" service.

Far Niente Ⓢ *Continental* — — — | VE

Financial District | 187 Bay St. (Wellington St.) | 416-214-9922

Following an elaborate redo in 2006, this Financial District veteran draws praise for a "contemporary" new design that diners describe as more "upscale" and "much more comfortable" than before; chef Gordon Mackie's Continental menu delivers some "delicious flavour combinations" and the "professional" staff "takes good care of customers", making this neighbourhood stalwart an always "reliable" option for a "power lunch."

Fat Cat Bistro Ⓢⓜ *French* | 25 | 18 | 24 | $68

Forest Hill | 376 Eglinton Ave. W. (Avenue Rd.) | 416-484-4228 | www.fatcat.ca

"One of Toronto's best-kept secrets", Mathew Sutherland's dinner-only New French bistro in Forest Hill provides "a gourmet experience" with "neighbourhood flair" ("I can't believe such fantastic food can come out of a kitchen so small"); a "superior wine list" and almost "flawless" service are big pluses, but the "charming" room seats only 34, so be sure to make a reservation.

	FOOD	DECOR	SERVICE	COST

Ferro Bar & Cafe *Italian/Pizza*

| 21 | 15 | 16 | $43 |

Hillcrest-Davenport | 769 St. Clair Ave. W. (Arlington Ave.) |
416-654-9119 | www.ferrobarcafe.ca

"Huge servings" of "lovely" Southern Italian eats (especially "fabulous" wood-fired pizza) plus "very fair prices" equal "always crowded" conditions at this "funky" cafe in the Hillcrest-Davenport area; "harried staffers" have to navigate among "close-together tables" and it's "so loud you might as well be eating on a runway", but undaunted *amici* assert this "great little spot" remains a "favourite."

Fifth Grill, The ⌧Ⓜ *Steak*

| – | – | – | VE |

Entertainment District | 225 Richmond St. W. (Duncan St.) |
416-979-3005 | www.thefifthgrill.com

Reopened in April 2006, this former warehouse in the Entertainment District has adopted a pricey à la carte steakhouse menu, offering cuts of beef topped with luxe flourishes like half a lobster tail; in the dining room, modern elements (e.g. Parsons chairs) update a country French-inspired setting; N.B. open Thursday–Saturday for dinner only.

Five Doors North ⌧ *Italian*

| 20 | 12 | 18 | $43 |

Midtown | 2088 Yonge St. (bet. Davisville & Eglinton Aves.) | 416-480-6234 |
www.fivedoorsnorth.com

"The type of place you'd go with a crowd", this "boisterous" and "unpretentious" Midtown Italian serves up an eclectic menu of "homestyle" fare ("sauce that tastes like my nonna's") in a "quirky" room lit by mismatched "lamps hanging on their sides"; "friendly", "relaxed" service helps make an evening here "feel like an event."

Flow Restaurant & Lounge *Eclectic*

| 17 | 22 | 17 | $66 |

Bloor Yorkville | 133 Yorkville Ave. (Avenue Rd.) | 416-925-2143 |
www.flowrestaurant.com

At this Bloor Yorkville Eclectic, contemporary decor helps foster a "trendy" "people-watching" scene where "yuppies" savour "small dishes" with "big flavours" along with a few of the 300 wines; however, plenty dub this place "mediocre for the price" given "below-par" service and food that "doesn't meet expectations."

Fresh *Vegetarian*

| 20 | 15 | 15 | $23 |

Annex | 326 Bloor St. W. (Spadina Ave.) | 416-531-2635

(continued)

(continued)

Fresh

Queen West | 147 Spadina Ave. (bet. Queen & Richmond Sts.) | 416-599-4442
Queen West Gallery District | 894 Queen St. W. (Crawford St.) | 416-913-2720
www.juiceforlife.com

This trio of vegetarian "juice bars" nurtures a "granola-eating, tree-hugging" clientele with a "creative" "selection of sin-free dishes" that are "healthy yet delicious"; "high-design" "cafe ambience" contrasts with "enthusiastic" staffers sporting "dreadlocks, tattoos and piercings"; N.B. the Annex location recently moved a few blocks east.

Fressen *Vegetarian*   20 | 19 | 15 | $36

Queen West | 478 Queen St. W. (bet. Bathurst St. & Spadina Ave.) | 416-504-5127 | www.fressenrestaurant.com

"Those who can live without meat" come to this Queen West eatery to graze on the "flavourful" and "creative" vegan/vegetarian victuals of aptly named chef-owner Steven Gardner; the "hushed" earth-toned room "looks like a forest" to boot, but "service can be slow."

Fune *Japanese*   20 | 16 | 18 | $56

Entertainment District | 100 Simcoe St. (Adelaide St. W.) | 416-599-3868

A 2005 redo rendered this Entertainment District Japanese "more up-scale" without eliminating its "charming" sushi bar, a curved 28-seat counter where servings of "fresh, succulent" rolls "float by on little boats"; for patrons sitting at tables, "attentive" staffers ferry the fare.

Fusilli Ⓢ *Italian*   21 | 19 | 21 | $37

Corktown | 531 Queen St. E. (River St.) | 416-214-5148

This rustic, "checked-tablecloth" Southern Italian nook in Corktown pleases paesani with the namesake pasta, veal dishes and other "solid", "plentiful" *cucina*; rotating displays of work by local artists heighten the "cosy", "cheerful" ambience.

NEW Fuzion Ⓜ *Eclectic*   - | - | - | E

Downtown Core | 580 Church St. (bet. Gloucester & Wellesley Sts.) | 416-944-9888 | www.fuzionexperience.com

Set in a converted Victorian mansion, this Downtown Core Eclectic offers a seasonal, seafood-heavy menu from toque Patrick Weise (former personal chef to Oprah Winfrey); the dining room is trendy yet romantic, the lounge serves up signature cocktails and weekend DJs, and the backyard garden with its fish pond and waterfall is ideal for special events; N.B. dinner-only.

Gallery Grill Canadian

24 | 25 | 24 | $48

South Annex | Hart House | 7 Hart House Circle (Wellesley St.) | 416-978-2445 | www.gallerygrill.com

Ensconced in the University of Toronto's historic Hart House, this "tranquil" yet "convivial" neo-Gothic dining room and lounge offers academia-lovers the opportunity to eat lunch or Sunday brunch amid "ivory tower perfection"; "talented chef" Suzanne Baby turns out "delicate, exciting" Canadian cuisine ("local produce adds to the vigour") that's "swiftly" served by a "gracious" staff; N.B. closed Saturdays.

Gamelle ⑤ French

22 | 19 | 22 | $66

Little Italy | 468 College St. (bet. Bathurst & Markham Sts.) | 416-923-6254 | www.gamelle.com

At this "welcoming" "French oasis in the Little Italy mix", the "fine" "traditional" bistro fare is "a labour of love" served by an "attentive" crew; the "comfy" spot with de rigueur framed posters has an "intimate, charming" feel that makes it "perfect" for a "slow lunch" ("leave the office and don't come back"); P.S. sit on the "lovely back patio" if possible.

⦿ George ⑤ Canadian

26 | 24 | 24 | $87

Downtown Core | Queen Richmond Ctr. | 111C Queen St. E. (bet. Church & Jarvis Sts.) | 416-863-6006 | www.georgeonqueen.com

By George, it's "amazing" assert admirers of this onetime chocolate factory in the Downtown Core's Queen Richmond Centre; "master chef" Lorenzo Loseto's "flavourful", seasonal Canadian cuisine comes on "small plates [that] allow for maximum sampling" and can be paired with three- or six-oz. pours; the antique "industrial" open-plan setting manages to be both "stylish" and "soothing", helped along by "smooth, accommodating service."

Gio Rana's Really
Really Nice Restaurant Ⓜ Italian

23 | 17 | 23 | $54

Leslieville | 1220 Queen St. E. (Leslie St.) | 416-469-5225

Set in a converted bank building in Leslieville with a "mismatched" and deconstructed decor, this Italian draws "a fun, mixed crowd" seeking "unpretentious", "reasonably priced" "home cooking" and "tapas-style delights" served by a "charming staff"; keep in mind: "terrible acoustics" make it "too loud for conversation" and there's no official sign (although Gio's enormous schnoz sculpture hangs over the door); N.B. they've recently expanded into an adjacent building.

NEW Globe Bistro *Eclectic*

– | – | – | VE

Danforth-Greektown | 124 Danforth Ave. (Broadview Ave.) | 416-466-2000 | www.globebistro.com

They're thinking globally and acting locally at this Danforth addition where the Eclectic menu features a pricey mix of molecular gastronomy (e.g. rib-eye with Ermite blue cheese foam) and regionally sourced, farm-fresh food; it's all paired with an extensive vino list and served in a hip setting highlighted by 16-ft. ceilings, an open kitchen and a wine bar; N.B. a jazz vocalist entertains on Wednesday nights.

grano ⑤ *Italian*

19 | 17 | 19 | $49

Midtown | 2035 Yonge St. (bet. Davisville & Eglinton Aves.) | 416-440-1986 | www.grano.ca

Amici adore "choosing their own appetizers" from an "unbelievable antipasto bar", then digging into the entrees at this "lively", "rustic" Midtown trattoria; while the local clientele "discusses the state of the world with animated friends", the husband-and-wife owners "make everyone feel like family"; N.B. serves breakfast.

Grappa Ristorante Ⓜ *Italian*

20 | 16 | 21 | $51

Little Italy | 797 College St. (Ossington Ave.) | 416-535-3337

Appreciated for a "laid-back staff" that's "as attentive to the fussy eight-year-old as it is to the gourmet professor", this "convivial" Little Italy ristorante has proven itself to be a "steady performer" proffering "reliably fine" "down-home Italian food" along with some 250 wines; it may not be fancy, but this "cosy", "comfortable joint" nevertheless "stands out."

Ⓩ Harbour Sixty Steakhouse *Steak*

25 | 23 | 22 | $101

Harbourfront | Toronto Harbour Commission Bldg. | 60 Harbour St. (Bay St.) | 416-777-2111 | www.harboursixty.com

To "celebrate special occasions" – e.g. "a Leafs victory" at the nearby Air Canada Centre – well-heeled carnivores come to this Harbourfront spot for "slabs of meat" that are "cooked to perfection" and "generous sides" ordered à la carte; the "engaging" "old gentlemen's club setting" in a historic "port office building" and "excellent" if "snooty" service – not to mention "large price tags" on food and wine – make it an "expense-account favourite."

Hemispheres *Eclectic* | 23 | 20 | 21 | $82 |

Downtown Core | Metropolitan Hotel | 110 Chestnut St. (bet. Bay St. & University Ave.) | 416-599-8000 | www.metropolitan.com
Partisans who praise this Downtown Core Eclectic's "creative" "Asian-infused dishes" and 250-label wine list also express their admiration for the generally "attentive" service; expect an "enjoyable" "business-lunch ambience", even if the glass-and-brick setting at the Metropolitan makes it all too clear you're dining "in a 1980s-style hotel."

Herbs Ⓜ *French* | 22 | 17 | 20 | $65 |

North Toronto | 3187 Yonge St. (Lawrence Ave.) | 416-322-0487 | www.herbsrestaurant.com
A North Toronto "neighbourhood fixture", this New French remains a "reliable choice" for locals who laud its "fresh-from-the-garden" fare; "sparkling waiters" provide "attentive service" in the "cheery" environs, and though solo diners "often wind up here", families report it's "child-friendly" as well (and therefore "a little loud").

Z Hiro Sushi Ⓢ Ⓜ *Japanese* | 27 | 15 | 21 | $72 |

St. Lawrence | 171 King St. E. (Jarvis St.) | 416-304-0550
Hiro worshipers say "sitting at the sushi bar is the only way to experience" this small, traditional St. Lawrence Japanese; they adore the "genius" chef-owner's "amazing" omakase (a culinary "walk on the wild side") but caution that since "you'll eat at the master's pace" you may spend "a few hours" here.

Holt Renfrew Cafe *French* | 20 | 19 | 16 | $35 |

Bloor Yorkville | Holt Renfrew | 50 Bloor St. W. (bet. Bay & Yonge Sts.) | 416-922-2333 | www.holtrenfrew.com
For a "shopping break", "ladies who lunch" pop into this French "oasis" in Bloor Yorkville's ritzy Holt Renfrew department store; remodelled in 2005, the "ultramodern", "upscale cafe" specializes in "creative but pricey" tartines made with "bread flown in from France"; N.B. hours vary with the store's closing time.

	FOOD	DECOR	SERVICE	COST

Host, The *Indian*

23 | 19 | 19 | $39

Annex | 14 Prince Arthur Ave. (bet. Avenue Rd. & Bedford St.) | 416-962-4678
Mississauga | 33 City Centre Dr. (Hurontario St./Hwy. 10) | 905-566-4678
Richmond Hill | 670 Hwy. 7 E. (E. Beaver Creek Rd.) | 905-709-7070
www.welcometohost.com

This "respected" chainlet earns a host of compliments for its "fresh, delicious" and "authentic" Indian eats ("fabulous curries", "melt-in-your-mouth naan") served in "ethnic" environs; while surveyors are split on service ("officious" vs. "infrequently attentive") and some prices may be "higher" than competitors', the "reasonable lunch buffet" is "well worth" the cost.

House of Chan *Chinese/Steak*

21 | 8 | 17 | $79

Forest Hill | 876 Eglinton Ave. W. (west of Bathurst St.) | 416-781-5575 | www.houseofchan.ca

A "Toronto landmark" serving both Chinese chow and prime steaks since 1960, this "dark", "old-school" Forest Hill "joint" inspires feedback as divided as its "bifurcated personality": devotees laud "excellent" chops and "lobsters the size of Chicago" proffered by a "friendly staff", while critics call it "a shadow of its former self", with "overpriced" eats and "uneven service."

Hy's Steakhouse *Steak*

22 | 22 | 22 | $79

Financial District | 120 Adelaide St. W. (bet. Bay & York Sts.) | 416-364-3326 | www.hyssteakhouse.com

Hy rollers and their "cronies" in the Financial District hang out at this "old-fashioned steakhouse" (part of a national chain), a "sentimental favourite" for "good but not world-class" chops; "obliging" servers do their thing as patrons "relax" by the hearth in the "gorgeously restored, high-ceilinged former bank building"; N.B. the bar is "great for drinks" "or something else" after work.

▣ Il Fornello *Italian/Pizza*

18 | 16 | 17 | $38

Bayview Village | Bayview Village Shopping Ctr. | 2901 Bayview Ave. (Sheppard Ave.) | 416-227-1271
Church & Wellesley | 491 Church St. (bet. Maitland & Wellesley Sts.) | 416-944-9052
Danforth-Greektown | 576 Danforth Ave. (bet. Carlaw & Pape Aves.) | 416-466-2931
Entertainment District | 214 King St. W. (Simcoe St.) | 416-977-2855 ▣

FOOD | DECOR | SERVICE | COST

(continued)

Il Fornello

Harbourfront | Queen's Quay Terminal | 207 Queen's Quay W. (York St.) | 416-861-1028

Midtown | 1560 Yonge St. (Delisle Ave.) | 416-920-7347

Oakville | Abbey Ctr. | 203 N. Service Rd. W. (Dorval Dr.) | 905-338-5233

Richmond Hill | 8851 Yonge St. (Hwy. 7) | 905-530-1153

The Beach | 2022 Queen St. E. (Waverly Rd.) | 416-691-8377

www.ilfornello.com

"Excellent", "reliable" "thin-crust pizza" and other "respectable" eats render this "Everyman's" Italian chain a "family-friendly" "value" that "caters to many dietary needs"; decor varies a bit by location but all are "decent" (if "formulaic"), making them "staples" for those seeking "a fast cheap bite."

Il Mulino *Italian*

26 | 20 | 24 | $75

Forest Hill | 1060 Eglinton Ave. W. (Bathurst St.) | 416-780-1173 | www.ilmulinorestaurant.com

Bolstered by a "magnificent wine list" to "suit every taste and budget", the "innovative" *cucina* at this "outstanding" Forest Hill Italian evokes "trips to Tuscany"; *amici* also adore "friendly" staffers and owners who "greet you like family", so although the simple 65-seat room with vaulted ceiling can get "noisy", locals' "only complaint is that more people are getting to know about it."

Il Posto *Italian*

21 | 20 | 21 | $67

Bloor Yorkville | 148 Yorkville Ave. (Avenue Rd.) | 416-968-0469 | www.ilposto.ca

"Quality" Italian classics and "warm", "smooth service" satisfy surveyors at this "sophisticated" Bloor Yorkville old-timer, a "tranquil oasis" offering "romantic" outdoor dining "in a courtyard by Hazelton Lanes"; it's "convenient" "for business lunches" as well; N.B. an ownership change may outdate the above scores.

Indian Rice Factory *Indian*

21 | 17 | 18 | $46

Annex | 414 Dupont St. (Howland Ave.) | 416-961-3472 | www.indianricefactory.com

"For many years", say supporters, this "celebrated" Annex Indian has provided "tasty", "refined" cuisine in a "pretty", "contemporary environment" (the patio "with fountain" and flowers evokes "a country garden"); nevertheless, a "disappointed" minority dubs the food "overpriced" and the portions "small", declaring that this veteran's "day of greatness is past."

Izakaya *Japanese*

| 19 | 24 | 19 | $32 |

St. Lawrence | 69 Front St. E. (Church St.) | 416-703-8658 | www.izakaya.ca

Incongruously set in a 1796 building in historic St. Lawrence, this "hip", "modern" Japanese noodle house with "cool communal tables" and a "calm ambience" feels like a "small slice of Tokyo"; "decent" (and "cheap") "made-to-order" bowls of soba and udon plus imported sakes, beers and Asian liquors are served by "friendly" folks who "seem to enjoy themselves"; N.B. no sushi.

Jacques' Bistro du Parc *French*

| 22 | 15 | 25 | $48 |

Bloor Yorkville | 126A Cumberland St. (bet. Avenue Rd. & Bay St.) | 416-961-1893

Owners Jacques and Martine Sorin "couldn't be nicer" and "service is always excellent" aver *amis* of this Bloor Yorkville bistro that "makes the simple [French] classics sing in a way that makes you understand why they're classics"; the Provençal-style room feels "intimate" and "charming" despite (or perhaps because of) "its humble demeanour."

NEW Jamie Kennedy at the Gardiner *Canadian*

| – | – | – | E |

Bloor Yorkville | Gardiner Museum | 111 Queen's Park, 3rd fl. (Bloor St.) | 416-362-1957 | www.jamiekennedy.ca

The recently renovated Gardiner Museum in Bloor Yorkville is the site of celebrity chef Jamie Kennedy's latest venture, this airy dining room inspired by the Pacific Northwest and offering a daily changing menu of seasonal Canadian fare along with a few global selections; the cuisine is complemented by an all-Ontario wine list, and while the venue is lunch-only Saturday–Thursday, it extends its hours on Fridays to serve a $49 three-course prix fixe dinner menu.

☑ Jamie Kennedy Wine Bar & Restaurant *Canadian/French*

| 25 | 21 | 21 | $63 |

St. Lawrence | 9 Church St. (south of Front St.) | 416-362-1957 | www.jamiekennedy.ca

"Superstar" chef Jamie Kennedy's "legions of fans" laud his "fabulous" conjoined Canadian-French eateries in St. Lawrence; the open-kitchen wine bar "churns out" "explosively flavourful" small plates for pairing with "outstanding" vintages "often unavailable elsewhere", while the "small", minimalist restaurant also offers "superb bistro fare" served by a "knowledgeable" crew with a touch of "attitude"; not surprisingly, this "finger food [comes] at full torso prices."

Jerusalem *Mideastern* `20` `11` `16` `$32`
Bayview Village | 4775 Leslie St. (bet. Finch & Sheppard Aves.) | 416-490-7888
Forest Hill | 955 Eglinton Ave. W. (Bathurst St.) | 416-783-6494
www.jerusalemrestaurant.com
"Authentic" Middle Eastern eats and "low prices" add up to "value" at this no-frills Forest Hill "institution"; most find the staff "friendly" and the scene "pleasant", but dissenters urge "get it to go"; N.B. the Bayview Village branch has lunch and dinner buffets.

Joso's ⓩ *Seafood* `24` `19` `21` `$73`
Annex | 202 Davenport Rd. (Avenue Rd.) | 416-925-1903 | www.josos.com
"A feast for your eyes and your palate", this "great family-run" Annex seafooder turns the "freshest" catch of the day into "spectacular grilled" fish dishes served in a bi-level "temple celebrating the female form" (translation: painted and sculpted "breasts abound"); frequent celeb spottings provide additional "eye candy", and "solid" service is "an unexpected plus."

JOV Ⓜ *French* `25` `19` `22` `$77`
Leaside | 1701 Bayview Ave. (1 block south of Eglinton Ave. W.) | 416-322-0530 | www.jovbistro.com
"Take a risk with the tasting menu – you won't be disappointed" urge surveyors smitten by this 40-seat New French in Leaside, where "fabulous" chef Masayuki Tamaru takes diners on a culinary "adventure"; plus, the "cosy" mirrored room is "buzzing with energy" and peopled by a "friendly, helpful" staff.

ⓩ Jump Café & Bar ◑ⓩ *American* `21` `20` `21` `$68`
Financial District | Commerce Ct. E. | 18 Wellington St. W. (bet. Bay & Yonge Sts.) | 416-363-3400 | www.jumpcafe.com
There's no leap of faith required at this "always reliable" Financial District "fixture" – an Oliver Bonacini (Canoe, Auberge du Pommier) "power-lunch" "mainstay" where a "solid kitchen" turns out "thought-

ful" New American fare (including "amazing" specials) served by a "fast", "friendly" crew; the high-ceilinged, marble-floored space can seem "noisy", but it's "less deafening away from the bar area."

NEW kaiseki-SAKURA *Japanese*

| - | - | - | VE |

Downtown Core | 556 Church St. (Wellesley St.) | 416-923-1010 | www.kaisekisakura.com

Those who love Japanese cuisine will appreciate this Downtown Core temple to *kaiseki*-style small plates, where chef Daisuke Izutsu offers monthly changing tasting menus that range from five to eight courses ($60–$100); a relative secret, this dinner-only destination also serves intricate, artfully presented à la carte choices in a quiet setting that's ideal for relaxed conversation; N.B. closed on Tuesdays.

Kalendar ● *Eclectic*

| - | - | - | I |

Little Italy | 546 College St. (Euclid Ave.) | 416-923-4138 | www.kalendar.com

For a late-night bite in Little Italy, try this hip, casual College Street spot where an affordable Eclectic menu is highlighted by a variety of 'scrolls' (crêpe-style stuffed rotis) and 'nannettes' (naan bread bearing pizza-esque toppings); a large selection of specialty martinis suits the twentysomething crowd just fine, as does prime people-watching from the street-facing patio.

Katsura *Japanese*

| 22 | 20 | 21 | $57 |

Don Mills | Westin Prince Hotel | 900 York Mills Rd. (Don Mills Rd.) | 416-444-2511 | www.katsurarestaurant.com

"Try to get seated at a cooking table" to "enjoy the show" by the "real teppanyaki chefs" at this "old favourite" located in the Westin Prince Hotel in Don Mills; the "tableside fun" adds a flourish to the "reliable" "traditional" Japanese fare (including "always fresh sushi") and compensates for the somewhat "understated" decor; P.S. "Sunday night dinner specials" are "the best deal."

Ki ●⊠ *Japanese*

| 21 | 24 | 19 | $82 |

Financial District | BCE Pl. | 181 Bay St. (Wellington St.) | 416-308-5888 | www.kijapanese.com

A "modern"-Asian expanse in the Financial District, this "sumptuous" restaurant "never feels crowded even when full" – which it often is, given its Bay Street location; "power brokers" and "beautiful people" come by to "drink martinis" and down "small portions" of "varied"

FOOD DECOR SERVICE COST

Japanese fare served by "eager-to-please" staffers, while wallet-watchers sigh "boy, does it add up quickly"; N.B. serves till midnight.

Korea House ● *Korean* | 21 | 10 | 18 | $29 |

Koreatown | 666 Bloor St. W. (Manning Ave.) | 416-536-8666
"Authentic" Seoul food ("excellent grilled meat", "delish side plates", "dynamite kimchi") attracts admirers to this "tried-and-true" Koreatown "favourite"; they're deterred neither by a "chintzy", "tired" setting nor by occasionally "sporadic" service.

NEW Kultura Social Dining *Eclectic* | – | – | – | E |

Downtown Core | 169 King St. E. (bet. George & Jarvis Sts.) | 416-363-9000 | www.kulturarestaurant.com
Delivering small plates that are big on taste and creativity, this ultra-romantic Downtown Core restaurant offers an Eclectic menu from chef/co-owner Roger Mooking that reveals his Caribbean and Japanese roots in dishes like jerk chicken with a lemon and coconut risotto; it's already attracting a business and celebrity clientele that's likely to appreciate the deft wine list (with 50 selections by the glass) from noted Canadian sommelier Kim Cyr.

La Bruschetta ⚅ *Italian* | 22 | 13 | 23 | $44 |

Corso Italia | 1317 St. Clair Ave. W. (Lansdowne Ave.) | 416-656-8622
The "charismatic" owners of this "family-run" Corso Italia trattoria act like "everyone's their best friend" as they serve up "homemade" pastas ("best-in-the-city" gnocchi) and "excellent appetizers"; the "old-fashioned" setup could use some "new energy", but its overall charm "keeps the celebrities coming back"; N.B. recent renovations may outdate the above Decor score.

La Fenice ⚅ *Italian* | 21 | 16 | 21 | $61 |

Entertainment District | 319 King St. W. (bet. John & Peter Sts.) | 416-585-2377 | www.lafenice.ca
Aptly named for Venice's famous opera house, this Entertainment District Italian is "good for a pre-theatre meal" given its "excellent" *cucina* (including a "great selection" of "fresh fish"), strong regional wine list and "efficient" service; at midday, it turns into a "crowded" and "dependable" "corporate lunching ground" "with something for everyone"; the sole sour note: "bland" interiors ("so much marble you think you're eating in a mausoleum").

	FOOD	DECOR	SERVICE	COST

NEW Lai Toh Heen M *Chinese*   - | - | - | E

Midtown | 692 Mount Pleasant Rd. (Soudan Ave.) | 416-489-8922 | www.laitohheen.com

Offering upscale Chinese cuisine in an elegant, art deco setting in Midtown, this sibling of Lai Wah Heen delivers an artful selection of dim sum along with creative à la carte dishes; in the evenings, the well-heeled clientele can opt for a six- or eight-course tasting menu ($70 and $90, respectively); N.B. closed Mondays and Tuesdays.

Z Lai Wah Heen *Chinese*   27 | 22 | 25 | $68

Downtown Core | Metropolitan Hotel | 108 Chestnut St. (bet. Bay St. & University Ave.) | 416-977-9899 | www.metropolitan.com/lwh

Renowned for "divine" dim sum "made with tremendous care" and served similarly by a "top-notch" staff, this "superior" Sino in the Downtown Core's Metropolitan Hotel is likely to "make visitors from Hong Kong feel right at home"; dining in this "serene" "white-tablecloth" setting may be "expensive by Chinese standards" but it's "a bargain" for such "a wonderful experience."

Lakes *Continental/French*   20 | 16 | 20 | $69

Rosedale-Summerhill | 1112 Yonge St. (Roxborough St.) | 416-966-0185

"You know what to expect and you're likely to see someone you know" at this Rosedale-Summerhill "hangout" according to locals who happily dive into its "upscale" Continental-French cookery and "lovely selection of wines" (including nearly 50 half-bottles); "cosy, laid-back" and "comfortable", this is a "great neighbourhood place."

La Palette *French*   ▽ 23 | 13 | 17 | $44

Chinatown-Kensington | Kensington Mkt. | 256 Augusta Ave. (College St.) | 416-929-4900

When "strolling around Kensington Market", don't miss this "rowdy bistro" on the edge of Chinatown for "wonderful" French standards and "best-value" prix fixe dinners proffered by "informed, efficient" servers; the "thrift shop-style" dining room is "generally packed", so call ahead; N.B. a post-Survey chef change may outdate the Food score.

Z Lee Ⓢ *Asian Fusion/Mediterranean*   27 | 23 | 22 | $63

King West | 603 King St. W. (Portland St.) | 416-504-7867 | www.susur.com

The comparatively "affordable little sister" to next door's Susur, this King West "favourite" allows fans of "the master" to "get a taste" of

	FOOD	DECOR	SERVICE	COST

Susur Lee's "sensational", "surprising" Asian-Med "fusion food" ("tapas meets dim sum") "without breaking the bank"; the "stylish" loftlike space with pink Lucite tables is a "hip", "hopping" (if "chaotic") scene that's "good for groups", as is the new outdoor patio.

Lee Garden ● *Chinese*

| 23 | 12 | 18 | $32 |

Chinatown-Kensington | 331 Spadina Ave. (St. Andrews St.) | 416-593-9524

"Foodie snobs may pooh-pooh" this "classic" Mandarin in Chinatown-Kensington but "line-ups out the door" suggest it's at least "a notch above" nearby competitors thanks to "outstanding" "traditional" chow and "unpretentious service"; as a result, regulars don't care that it's comparatively "pricey", figuring that the bill won't "burn too big a hole in your pocket."

Le Paradis *French*

| 21 | 18 | 21 | $43 |

Annex | 166 Bedford Rd. (Davenport Rd.) | 416-921-0995 | www.leparadis.com

"Still going strong after all these years", this "sophisticated but simple" Annex bistro is "always busy and with good reason": namely, "reliable", moderately priced French "classics done very well" plus an "accessible" wine list with "low markups"; "warm yet not too obtrusive" service wins hearts but even fans admit the "decor needs a defibrillator"; P.S. though not required, reservations are a "must."

Le Sélect Bistro *French*

| 21 | 20 | 20 | $49 |

Entertainment District | 432 Wellington St. W. (Spadina Ave.) | 416-596-6405 | www.leselect.com

In January 2006, this "perennial favourite" relocated to "more spacious" digs in the Entertainment District – but fortunately the bistro's proprietors brought along the "French atmosphere" (including the original zinc bar but not the "trademark" hanging bread baskets), the "outstanding" 1,200-label wine collection and the "honest and delicious" Gallic goodies; "the move has got the staff's attention" too ("no longer on automatic" pilot).

🆕 Leslie Jones 🅼🏴 *Mediterranean*

| - | - | - | M |

Leslieville | 1182 Queen St. E. (bet. Jones Ave. & Leslie St.) | 416-463-5663 | www.lesliejones.ca

Keeping it simple with casual decor and homestyle eats, this cosy Leslieville addition is luring locals with its satisfying Med entrees and pastas; given its relaxed ambience and service and its quiet backyard patio, you may just feel like you're dining at a friend's place, with the music to match – the chef-owner favours Neil Young and Bob Dylan; N.B. it's cash-only and closed on Mondays and Tuesdays.

Le Trou Normand 🛛 *French* | 20 | 17 | 20 | $50 |

Bloor Yorkville | 90 Yorkville Ave. (bet. Avenue Rd. & Yonge St.) | 416-967-5956 | www.letrounormand.ca

"Unpretentious" and "sunny", this Bloor Yorkville spot gives "good value for the money" assert patrons pleased by the "warm service" and "traditional" Gallic fare cooked up by a chef who's been here for more than 30 years; however, modernists moan the interior "needs a lot of refreshing" and the menu's passé ("even the French don't eat like this anymore").

Lobby 🛛Ⓜ *Eclectic* | 19 | 25 | 15 | $70 |

Bloor Yorkville | 192 Bloor St. W. (bet. Avenue & Bedford Rds.) | 416-929-7169 | www.eatdrinkplay.ca

A "happening" "place for drinks" and "beautiful-people-watching", this Bloor Yorkville venue evokes the public spaces of a boutique hotel – complete with an on-site art gallery – with its recently renovated but still "satisfyingly trendy" digs; nevertheless, some patrons are less pleased with the "overpriced" Eclectic fare and "slow" service; N.B. a post-Survey chef change may outdate the above Food score.

Lolita's Lust *Mediterranean* | 21 | 16 | 16 | $61 |

Danforth-Greektown | 513 Danforth Ave. (bet. Carlaw & Logan Aves.) | 416-465-1751 | www.lolitaslust.ca

Admirers of this "funky", "sexy" Med in Danforth-Greektown lust after its "eclectic" menu of "snack-sized plates" (a "nice break" from the Hellenics hereabouts) and find it a "haven" thanks to "secluded booths", a fireplace for winter and floor-to-ceiling doors that open to admit summer breezes; still, critics call the servers "haughty" and claim it's "hard to warm to" the "Berlin Wall decor."

Marcel's 🛛Ⓜ *French* | 20 | 17 | 19 | $53 |

Entertainment District | 315 King St. W. (bet. John & Peter Sts.) | 416-591-8600 | www.marcels.com

"Geared to theatregoers", this "reliable" French in the Entertainment District is "popular" and convenient for a "quick bite" pre-curtain; reviews are mixed, however, with fans applauding "spot-on" cuisine delivered "with panache" and critics panning "uninspiring" eats, decor that's "neither here nor there" and "variable" service.

Matignon 🖪 *French*

| 22 | 20 | 27 | $56 |

Downtown Core | 51 St. Nicholas St. (Yonge St.) | 416-921-9226 | www.matignon.ca

Patrons are pampered by "warm", "well-paced", "attentive but not intrusive" service at this "inviting" bistro in the Downtown Core; what's more, its "delightful" French standards are "filled with terrific flavour" ("great" prix fixe options) and presented "with flair", making this "small" and "often overlooked gem" "well worth repeat visits."

NEW MEATing 🖪 *Steak*

| - | - | - | VE |

Midtown | 2411 Yonge St. (bet. Broadway & Roselawn Aves.) | 416-487-8609 | www.meating.com

As its name implies, this Midtown sibling of the neighbouring Cfood caters to carnivores with its menu of 'tame', 'game' and 'organic' meats ranging from lamb chop to kangaroo; it attracts a twentysomething crowd that feels right at home amid mod green-and-brown decor (check out the acrylic moose head); N.B. be sure to top off your meal with a huge, $20 slice of Operation Herbie cake, the proceeds of which go to The Hospital for Sick Children.

Merlot *French*

| 20 | 17 | 19 | $57 |

Islington-Kingsway | 2994 Bloor St. W. (bet. Humbervale Blvd. & Royal York Rd.) | 416-236-0081

Islington-Kingsway locals raise their glasses to this "great" bistro, a "quaint" spot for "down-home French country cooking" ("all that's needed to make it authentic is a Gauloise-induced haze"); "tables are a bit close" together, so if the "wine-soaked din" proves too much, take your conversation out to the patio.

Messis *French*

| 23 | 18 | 21 | $51 |

South Annex | 97 Harbord St. (Spadina Ave.) | 416-920-2186 | www.messis.ca

"Great value" makes this "festive", "upscale" chef-owned New French in South Annex a "local favourite", with "imaginative and delicious" preparations ("wonderful grilled fish") proffered by a "pleasant" staff; the "contemporary yet warm" dining room and "lovely", "sleek" patio are usually "comfortably crowded" with a largely "over-40 clientele."

	FOOD	DECOR	SERVICE	COST

NEW Milagro ⑤ *Mexican* — — — E

Downtown Core | The Rosemount | 5 Mercer St. (John St.) | 416-850-2855 |
www.milagrorestaurant.com

Harkening back to an art deco–era cantina, this Downtown Core
Mexican run by two foodie brothers from Mexico City features authentic,
upscale cuisine in a high-ceilinged dining room punctuated with dark
wood and colourful accents; there's also a ceviche bar with a view into
the display kitchen, a focused wine list and a lengthy tequila selection.

Mildred Pierce *French* — 25 24 23 $64

King West | 99 Sudbury St. (bet. Dovercourt Rd. & Lisgar St.) | 416-588-5695 |
www.mildredpierce.com

"Once you finally find" this "oasis" in an "obscure industrial" part of King
West, "you'll be rewarded" with "superb" Med- and Asian-accented
French fare (including a "sophisticated" Sunday brunch) that "would
cost twice as much" elsewhere; the "nouveau-monde-meets-
Hollywood" dining room is augmented by an "English-garden-like" patio,
while the staffers "hover without making it seem like they are hovering."

Miller Tavern *Seafood* — 18 20 17 $58

York Mills | 3885 Yonge St. (York Mills St.) | 416-322-5544 | www.themiller.ca
Relax on the "lovely" patio ("like sitting in a California vineyard") at
this "historic inn" in York Mills, now an "upscale setting" for "revelry"
and "reliably" "good seafood"; though some shrug it's essentially a
"high-end pub" that's "too expensive for the neighbourhood", it nevertheless "always feels comfortable."

Millie's Bistro *Mediterranean* — 22 16 22 $50

North Toronto | 1980 Avenue Rd. (bet. Felbrigg & Haddington Aves.) |
416-481-1247

"Exotic food" and "casual dining" mix at this North Toronto Med where
the kitchen conjures up an "interesting" veg-friendly menu based on
"fresh ingredients" and "friendly" staffers help foster a "comfortable"
ambience for "convening with friends."

NEW Mirabelle ⑤ *European* — — — M

Midtown | 2112 Yonge St. (bet. Hillsdale Ave. & Manor Rd.) | 416-544-8700 |
www.mirabellewinebar.com

Taking its cue from Britain's trendy gastropubs, this 'gastro wine bar' in
Midtown proffers a range of sophisticated Modern European dishes ac-

companied by a solid vino list (including some 30 choices by the glass); it's all served with warmth and style in an airy dining room that some serious sippers may choose to spurn in favour of the comfortable lounge or the outdoor patio.

	FOOD	DECOR	SERVICE	COST
Mistura ⑆ *Italian*	25	24	24	$81

Annex | 265 Davenport Rd. (west of Avenue Rd.) | 416-515-0009 | www.mistura.ca

"Top drawer in all categories", this "heavenly" Annex Italian spotlights the "top-notch" cooking of mustachioed Massimo Capra ("a true character"); it's enhanced by "warm hospitality" from a "polished, gracious" staff whose "attention to detail" is evident throughout the "magically lit", "modern" yet "charming" room.

	FOOD	DECOR	SERVICE	COST
MoDo ⓜ *Italian*	-	-	-	E

Bloor Yorkville | 122-124 Avenue Rd. (Bernard Ave.) | 416-962-6636 | www.modotoronto.com

This Bloor Yorkville Italian focuses on tapaslike tasting plates served up in a dramatic room filled with texture (brick walls, plush chairs, velvety draperies); on weekends, you'll find jazz brunches as well as DJs and live music in the bar.

	FOOD	DECOR	SERVICE	COST
Moe Pancer's Delicatessen *Deli*	22	8	17	$24

Downsview | 3856 Bathurst St. (bet. Sheppard & Wilson Aves.) | 416-633-1230 | www.pancersdeli.com

Established in 1957 and relocated in 2004, this "old-school" Jewish deli "icon" in Downsview is "the undisputed corned beef king"; "beautiful" cured meats, "really sour dills" and "great potato salad" are among the "authentic" eats presented by a "quick, friendly" crew, although dated "diner"-esque decor has some recommending takeout ("eat at home, in the car or at the hotel").

	FOOD	DECOR	SERVICE	COST
Monsoon ⑆ *Asian Fusion*	21	23	20	$69

Entertainment District | 100 Simcoe St. (Adelaide St. W.) | 416-979-7172 | www.monsoonrestaurant.ca

Praise rains down on this "trendy" Entertainment District Asian fusion for its "ultrachic", "serene" interiors and its "high-quality" menu of Eastern eats that are also "prepared with a decorative flair"; the food comes to table courtesy of a "friendly" staff, but it can get "noisy", especially when occasional weekend DJs are in the house.

Morton's, The Steakhouse *Steak* | 23 | 20 | 23 | $81

Bloor Yorkville | Park Hyatt Hotel | 4 Avenue Rd. (Prince Arthur Ave.) | 416-925-0648 | www.mortons.com

"You know pretty much what to expect" here – this branch of the chophouse chain at Bloor Yorkville's Park Hyatt Hotel proffers "red meat extraordinaire" "cooked the way you like it the first time", bolstered by "fine wines" and served by a "top" crew in a "reliably manly" atmosphere; carnivores claim, however, that "T.O. has better steakhouses", while wallet-watchers warn "if the cholesterol doesn't kill you, the price of the sides will."

Nami ☒ *Japanese* | 24 | 18 | 21 | $59

St. Lawrence | 55 Adelaide St. E. (Yonge St.) | 416-362-7373 | www.namirestaurant.ca

The "grande dame of Toronto sushi", this St. Lawrence Japanese pleases fans with "well-executed" regional fare ranging from the raw ("amazing sushi pizza") to the cooked ("excellent" robata-grilled lobster, steak, vegetables and more); the main space is "typical" and, some say, "needs a makeover", but a "private tatami room completes the experience" quite handily.

Nataraj *Indian* | 20 | 10 | 15 | $34

Annex | 394 Bloor St. W. (Brunswick Ave.) | 416-928-2925 | www.nataraj.ca

Considered a "dependable favourite" by the "university crowd", this Annex Indian dishes out a "large variety" of "tasty" and "satisfying" subcontinental specialties that "aren't too spicy for most palates"; nevertheless, some surveyors sigh an "old-fashioned" interior and so-so service are "not impressive."

☒ North 44° ☒ *Continental* | 27 | 25 | 25 | $84

North Toronto | 2537 Yonge St. (Eglinton Ave.) | 416-487-4897 | www.north44restaurant.com

"Sophisticated" and "serene", Mark McEwan's North Toronto "showpiece" guarantees a "memorable" "special occasion" rave respondents, reporting the chef-owner's "magnificent" Continental cuisine evinces "superb quality and craftsmanship" while service is simply "state-of-the-art"; it's undoubtedly "pricey" and may be a "hassle to get to", but foodies urge their fellows to "walk, crawl, hitchhike . . . do whatever is necessary."

RESTAURANTS

	FOOD	DECOR	SERVICE	COST

NEW Opal Jazz Lounge ⌧ Ⓜ *French* — — — VE

Queen West West | 472 Queen St. W. (bet. Augusta Ave. & Portland St.) | 416-646-6725 | www.opaljazzlounge.com

This Queen West West newcomer doesn't miss a beat with its mix of live jazz, artful French cuisine and a solid wine list; it's all offered up in an urban-hip setting highlighted by a floor-to-ceiling image of Miles Davis and a piano that divides the space into a lounge and dining room (with no chair more than 10 yards from the action); N.B. there are two nightly seatings, at 6 PM and 9 PM.

Opus Restaurant ● *Continental* — 26 24 24 $87

Annex | 37 Prince Arthur Ave. (Bedford Rd.) | 416-921-3105 | www.opusrestaurant.com

"Discriminating" diners are "delighted" by this "top-notch" Annex veteran known for its "sublime" Continental cuisine and a "comprehensive" "wine book" (2,500 labels); "warm, sincere" staffers let you "take your time" in the brownstone's "formal" yet "soothing" monochromatic dining room or on the "lovely" atriumlike patio, making this a "great spot for a special occasion" (e.g. "impressing the in-laws").

⌧ Oro ⌧ *Mediterranean* — 27 22 26 $73

Downtown Core | 45 Elm St. (bet. Bay & Yonge Sts.) | 416-597-0155 | www.ororestaurant.com

"Somehow seeming out of the way while right in the middle of town", this "quiet" Downtown Core Med delivers with "exceptional", "innovative" cuisine ("melt-in-your-mouth calamari", "delectable desserts") as "attentive" owners circulate and "make everyone feel like family"; interiors are a "pleasantly odd mix" of "upscale" and retro, with three fireplaces adding both atmosphere and warmth ("first-class for a first date").

Oyster Boy *Seafood* — 23 15 20 $48

Queen West Gallery District | 872 Queen St. W. (bet. Crawford & Massey Sts.) | 416-534-3432 | www.oysterboy.ca

"Satisfy your oyster craving" or "stoke your libido" with an "excellent selection" of the beloved bivalves at this "casual" Queen West Gallery District mollusk mecca (which also offers fish 'n' chips and a "limited menu" of other "down-to-earth" dishes); "teeming with thirtysomethings", the "sociable" spot is "great" if you're "with a group"; N.B. it also offers weekend shucking classes.

	FOOD	DECOR	SERVICE	COST

Pangaea ⑤ Continental/Eclectic

| 25 | 23 | 23 | $74 |

Bloor Yorkville | 1221 Bay St. (Bloor St. W.) | 416-920-2323 | www.pangaearestaurant.com

"Celebrate a special occasion, win a client or dine with the family" at this "pampering" Bloor Yorkville Continental-Eclectic where the entrees are "simply prepared" yet "outstanding" ("supremely fresh seafood", "excellent mushroom risotto") and are bolstered by a "thoughtful" wine list and "sublime" desserts; "accommodating" servers lend added "calm" to this "chic" "oasis" (think "high ceilings and Mission-like" furnishings) "where you can hold a conversation without raising your voice."

Pan on the Danforth Greek

| 19 | 12 | 17 | $46 |

Danforth-Greektown | 516 Danforth Ave. (Ferrier St.) | 416-466-8158 | www.panonthedanforth.com

"There's more to Greek food" than souvlaki, as this "charming" Hellenic haunt proves via its more "modern" menu; proponents praise this Danforth-Greektown spot as a "step above the cookie-cutter" offerings elsewhere in the neighbourhood and salute "responsive" personnel, but critics pan the kitchen's "hit-and-miss" execution.

Pearl Harbourfront Chinese

| 21 | 18 | 18 | $43 |

Harbourfront | Queens Quay Terminal | 207 Queens Quay W. (York St.) | 416-203-1233 | www.pearlharbourfront.ca

"With a fantastic view (weather permitting)" of Lake Ontario from its "airy" space in "tourist-laden" Queens Quay Terminal, this Harbourfront Sino pleases both gazers and grazers; "delicious" dim sum is proffered by "attentive" servers "who remember you", so it's "typically crowded" for weekend brunch, even if some surveyors opine it's "overpriced" vis-à-vis Downtown's Chinatown.

Penrose Fish & Chips ⑤ⓜ Seafood

| 25 | 7 | 21 | $16 |

Midtown | 600 Mt. Pleasant Rd. (south of Eglinton Ave. E.) | 416-483-6800

"Seafood 'n' starch" (i.e. "exquisite fresh halibut and home-cut fries", deep-fried "in beef [drippings] for that authentic touch") have made this 40-seat Midtowner an "institution", and "friendly service by a caring family" helps to keep it that way; however, this "mainstay" is no-frills, which leads some to say they "prefer takeout"; N.B. closed during parts of July and/or August.

	FOOD	DECOR	SERVICE	COST

☑ Perigee ☒Ⓜ *French/Mediterranean* 27 | 23 | 25 | $115

Distillery District | Cannery Bldg. | 55 Mill St. (Trinity St.) | 416-364-1397 |
www.perigeerestaurant.com

For "pure theatre", "adventurous" gastronomes gather at this "fantastic"
French-Med in the historic Distillery District and settle into "arena-
side seats" by the open kitchen to be served a "blissful" blind tasting
menu; "social", "creative and charming" chef Pat Riley "explains each
course to you" amid converted industrial environs with thick wooden
beams and exposed brick; N.B. early birds and night owls can try pre-
theatre and dessert menus, respectively.

Peter's Chung King *Chinese* 21 | 4 | 16 | $26

Chinatown-Kensington | 281 College St. (west of Spadina Ave.) |
416-928-2936

"Zero atmosphere and who cares?" assert aficionados of this
Chinatown-Kensington "hole-in-the-wall" that turns out "cheap" and
"delicious" Szechuan eats ("perfectly balanced" hot-and-sour soup,
"especially good sizzling platters" plus "dishes you won't find elsewhere"); "waiters remember your favourites" and the vibe is "family-
friendly" so feel free to "bring the kids."

Phil's Original BBQ ☒ *BBQ* ∇ 22 | 9 | 18 | $25

Little Italy | 838 College St. (bet. Concord & Ossington Aves.) |
416-532-8161 | www.philsoriginalbbq.com

This Little Italy smoke shack serving specialties from south of the
Mason-Dixon line is known for "rib-sticking" 'cue ("try the pulled pork
sandwiches") that'll "satisfy your cravings"; no-frills decor is themat-
ically apt but one surveyor suggests true authenticity is still lacking: "I
asked if they had greens and the waitress thought I meant salad."

Pho Hung *Vietnamese* 20 | 7 | 13 | $16

Annex | 200 Bloor St. W. (Avenue Rd.) | 416-963-5080 ☒
Chinatown-Kensington | 350 Spadina Ave. (St. Andrews St.) |
416-593-4274 ⊐

"You don't go here for ambience", but these "authentic", "chaotic"
Vietnamese siblings in the Annex and Chinatown-Kensington offer
what may be the "best hangover cure in town" – "giant portions of
rare-beef noodles served with Vietnamese coffee" – plus "excellent pho"
and an array of other "fast, fresh and cheap" fare.

	FOOD	DECOR	SERVICE	COST

Pink Pearl *Chinese*

| | 19 | 15 | 18 | $38 |

Bloor Yorkville | 120 Avenue Rd. (Davenport Rd.) | 416-966-3631 | www.pink-pearl.ca

Surveyors say an "upscale" menu – including "excellent" midday dim sum – and a "convenient location" on the fringe of tony Bloor Yorkville are the sources of this "landmark" Cantonese's appeal; scores suggest solid service and decent decor, but not everybody approves of the exterior's "bizarre pink paint job."

Pony ⊠ *French*

| | 18 | 15 | 19 | $48 |

Little Italy | 488 College St. (Bathurst St.) | 416-923-7665 | www.ponyrestaurant.com

"Catering to a young crowd" with comparatively "affordable prices", this "intimate", "unpretentious" chef-owned bistro in Little Italy offers "always interesting", "always acceptable" French fusion fare ("stick with the specials") and a "lovely rooftop deck" ideal for a "romantic tête-à-tête"; P.S. the three-course prix fixe is a "great deal."

Positano ⓜ *Italian*

| | 22 | 16 | 23 | $51 |

Midtown | 633 Mt. Pleasant Rd. (Eglinton Ave. E.) | 416-932-3982

Thanks to "*delizioso* cucina, a "great wine list" and "friendly service" by "the loveliest people", locals claim this "family-run" Midtown Italian "stalwart" is "as authentic as you can get without a plane ticket"; although the 38-seat room admittedly seems "a bit cramped", dinner here is nevertheless a "truly outstanding value."

Prego Della Piazza *Italian*

| | 19 | 19 | 18 | $72 |

Bloor Yorkville | 150 Bloor St. W. (Avenue Rd.) | 416-920-9900 | www.pregodellapiazza.ca

The "see-and-be-seen" patio is a "magical place" "in the summer", but whatever the season, it's "always fun" to dine at this "lively" Bloor Yorkville Italian; a mixed clientele consisting of executives, shoppers and couples stops in for "tasty" if "not extraordinary" fare paired with vintages from an "excellent" list.

Provence Délices *Belgian/French*

| | - | - | - | M |

Cabbagetown | 12 Amelia St. (Parliament St.) | 416-924-9901 | www.provencerestaurant.com

Known for its weekend brunch, this Belgian-French stalwart in Cabbagetown serves a variety of hearty bistro standards (cassoulet, rabbit in mustard sauce) for lunch and dinner; its "airy", "unpretentious" dining room is accented with wood-burning stoves, French doors and full-grown trees, and there's a "super" outdoor patio too.

NEW Quince ◲ *Mediterranean* | - | - | - | M

Midtown | 2110 Yonge St. (bet. Hillsdale Ave. & Manor Rd.) | 416-488-2110 | www.quincerestaurant.ca

A varied menu keeps Midtowners coming back for more at this dinner-only Med addition offering entrees with French, Italian and Portuguese flair; a wood-burning oven adds depth to dishes like whole baked fish, and while the warm, inviting decor is a plus, it's the generous portions that are helping to make this an affordable choice.

Rain ◲ *Pan-Asian* | 24 | 26 | 22 | $95

Entertainment District | 19 Mercer St. (John St.) | 416-599-7246 | www.rainlounge.ca

Surveyors shower praise on the famously "trendy", "minimalist" interior design ("glowing" bar, circle-framed doorways, "indoor waterworks") of this Entertainment District "favourite", and the Pan-Asian small plates are lauded almost as loudly (tasting menus are "exceptional", signature miso black cod is "divinity in a mouthful"); while a few wet blankets dub the service "slow", sunnier sorts say the staff is "swift" and "knowledgeable."

Rodney's Oyster House ◖◲ *Seafood* | 24 | 17 | 20 | $65

King West | 469 King St. W. (Spadina Ave.) | 416-363-8105 | www.rodneysoysterhouse.com

Pescavores who are "in the mood for a little shuckin' and jivin'" drift over to this "casual" King West seafooder for "sensational oysters" and an array of "hearty" fin fare proffered without pretension (e.g. "water glasses for wine") by "sincere" folks; ok, the "kitschy" interior feels like being "in an old wooden boat", but even those who find the decor "disappointing" assert "your taste buds will thank you."

Rosebud, The *French* | - | - | - | E

Queen West West | 669 Queen St. W. (Markham St.) | 416-703-8810

Ideal for dining à deux, this charming, romantic bistro in the heart of Queen West West puts its own upscale stamp on classic French comfort food; the menu changes seasonally, but be prepared to wait in line-ups at all times of the year, as this cosy spot has just 35 seats.

	FOOD	DECOR	SERVICE	COST

☑ Ruth's Chris Steak House *Steak*
23 | **19** | **22** | **$78**

Downtown Core | Hilton Toronto | 145 Richmond St. W. (University Ave.) | 416-955-1455 | www.ruthschris.ca

"Butter plus steak equals pure gluttony" at this "meat eater's paradise", a link of the U.S. chain located in the Downtown Core's Hilton Toronto, where "sizzling", "succulent" slabs and "rich" sides in portions to "feed an army" are served by an "attentive" staff; even if some aesthetes deem the "dark", "subterranean convention-hall decor" "uninspiring", it remains a "classic" choice when using "the company expense account."

Salad King & Linda ☒ *Thai*
25 | **16** | **18** | **$21**

Downtown Core | 335 Yonge St. (Dundas St.) | 416-971-7041 | www.saladking.com

These Siamese twins in the Downtown Core conjure up "some of the best" "fiery, authentic Thai fare" in town; on the "cafeterialike" ground floor – an "always busy" "student haunt" where "long steel tables make for a communal feel" – the chow is "cheap" and line-ups "move fast" thanks to an "efficient" staff; if you prefer a more sedate, "less noisy" experience, opt for the "swankier upstairs" with "upscale" prices to match.

Savoy Bistro & Lounge ☒Ⓜ *French*
▽ **17** | **19** | **17** | **$57**

Downtown Core | 253 Victoria St. (Dundas Sq.) | 416-364-1013 | www.thesavoy.ca

This venue's "good" French fare and "consistent service" are slightly overshadowed by its "great atmosphere" and authentic Parisian decor (art deco lighting, enclosed booths); a Downtown Core location near the Canon Theatre makes it "easy before or after" a show.

☑ Scaramouche ☒ *Continental*
28 | **26** | **27** | **$95**

Forest Hill | 1 Benvenuto Pl. (bet. Avenue Rd. & Edmund St.) | 416-961-8011 | www.scaramoucherestaurant.com

Devotees of this "consistently" "top-notch" Forest Hill Continental declare its staff is "second to none" – indeed, surveyors voted this veteran Toronto's No. 1 for Service, citing "expert", "exquisite" ministrations that make you "feel like a millionaire" while chef/co-owner Keith Froggett feeds you his "delectable", "trustworthy, superb" cuisine; the "quiet, elegant" room is also renowned for "magnificent views of Downtown" ("without the Downtown traffic"), so "movers and shakers" recommend "lingering over a wonderful meal" to "savor" the "magic."

	FOOD	DECOR	SERVICE	COST

⛤ Scaramouche
Pasta Bar & Grill ◐⧄ *Italian*

27 | 25 | 27 | $68

Forest Hill | 1 Benvenuto Pl. (bet. Avenue Rd. & Edmund St.) | 416-961-8011 | www.scaramoucherestaurant.com

Sharing its Forest Hill building and "gorgeous views of Downtown", this "sophisticated sibling to Scaramouche" "continues to excel" as well, offering "lighter meals" of "marvellous" Italian *cucina* ("not just pasta") and "exceptional" service for a comparatively "reasonable price"; overall, it's a "more casual yet no less worthy" experience; N.B. the kitchen closes at midnight.

Senses Bakery & Restaurant ⧄Ⓜ *Eclectic*

24 | 20 | 22 | $73

Entertainment District | Soho Metropolitan Hotel | 328 Wellington St. W. (Blue Jays Way) | 416-935-0400 | www.senses.ca

Surveyors sense "brilliance" at this Eclectic in the Entertainment District's Soho Metropolitan Hotel thanks to the restaurant's "stunning" inventions and "playful interpretations of classic" dishes as well as the adjacent bakery's "fantastic" selection of lighter fare, cakes and tarts; it's all presented by "adept and enthusiastic" servers in a minimalist space that seems "chic" to some and "stark" to others; N.B. a post-Survey chef change may outdate the above Food score.

7 Numbers Ⓜ *Italian*

23 | 14 | 21 | $42

Danforth-Greektown | 307 Danforth Ave. (Bowden St.) | 416-322-5183 | www.sevennumbers.com

Serving up "fabulous" Southern Italian fare "just like mamma used to make", this "down-home" Danforth-Greektowner is run by a "great gang" that "treats regulars like family" – right down to "yelling at them for not finishing what's on their plates"; given the "funky" ambience and "dorm-room decor", canoodlers caution it may not be "your first choice for a romantic dinner."

Sher E Punjab *Indian*

23 | 15 | 21 | $33

Danforth-Greektown | 351 Danforth Ave. (Broadview Ave.) | 416-465-2125

An "Indian classic amidst the souvlaki houses" in Greektown, this "cosy" "old reliable" "full of students, academics" and local "lefties" offers a "variety" of "delicious" dishes ("a splash of flavour in your mouth"); "don't expect much" in the way of decor, but compensation comes in the form of "fine", "friendly service."

Smalltalk Bakery Cafe & Restaurant *French*　　　　▽ 23 | 17 | 18 | $47

Leaside | 1580 Bayview Ave. (Homefront Rd.) | 416-483-8400
The scuttlebutt on this "funky" Leaside bistro is that a "solid menu" of New French noshes makes it an "excellent spot for brunch" on weekends and an "appealing pit stop" on busy workdays as well; still, a finicky few feel the "staff needs training."

NEW Sopra Upper Lounge 🚭Ⓜ *Italian*　　- | - | - | E

Bloor Yorkville | 265 Davenport Rd. (bet. Avenue & Bedford Rds.) | 416-929-9006 | www.sopra.ca
Riding the wave of new jazz supper clubs, this swanky Bloor Yorkville addition makes a stylish entrance, offering an eclectic menu of Italian fare in a second-floor space designed for romance with its small, circular tables and sexy lighting; a backlit marble bar adds ambience, as does the nightly live entertainment: a pianist Tuesday–Wednesday and live bands Thursday–Saturday; N.B. dinner-only.

Sotto Sotto *Italian*　　　　　　　　　23 | 19 | 21 | $74

Bloor Yorkville | 116A Avenue Rd. (Davenport Rd.) | 416-962-0011
Sotto in the Village *Italian*
NEW Forest Hill | 425 Spadina Rd. (Lonsdale Rd.) | 416-322-8818
www.sottosotto.ca
"*Molto bene*" *cucina* brings boosters back to this "bustling", "belowground" Bloor Yorkville regional Italian where the pasta's "perfectly al dente", the wine list features "unique selections for those willing to splurge" and the "romantic" space has a "grottolike atmosphere"; though the presence of "visiting movie stars" makes for "great peoplewatching", some complain "the rest of us get treated like extras"; N.B. the equally upscale Sotto in the Village opened post-Survey.

NEW Spice Room & Chutney Bar *Eclectic*　　- | - | - | VE

Bloor Yorkville | Hazelton Lns. | 55 Avenue Rd. (Lowther Ave.) | 416-935-0000
Situated in trendy Bloor Yorkville, the latest from celebrity chef Greg Couillard puts spices front and centre on a compact yet creative Eclectic menu; while the bold, pricey fare tempts the palate, the romantic sand-and-black space (channeling a luxe tribal tent) delights the eyes; N.B. the Chutney Bar opens at noon and the Spice Room at 6 PM.

	FOOD	DECOR	SERVICE	COST

RESTAURANTS

☒ Splendido 🅼 *Mediterranean*   27 | 24 | 25 | $93

South Annex | 88 Harbord St. (Spadina Ave.) | 416-929-7788 |
www.splendidoonline.com

"Splendido indeed" rhapsodize respondents about this South Annex Med where chef David Lee's "sublime", "celestial" cuisine ("one of the city's best tasting menus") is complemented by an "impressive wine cellar" and served in a "classy", "modern", "clean"-lined dining room by a staff that offers a "perfect combination of professional and friendly" ministrations; "for a special occasion, you can't go wrong" here.

☒ Spring Rolls *Pan-Asian*   19 | 17 | 17 | $28

Downtown Core | 40 Dundas St. W. (Yonge St.) | 416-585-2929
Downtown Core | 693 Yonge St. (Bloor St.) | 416-972-6623
North Toronto | 45 Eglinton Ave. E. (Yonge St.) | 416-322-7655
St. Lawrence | 85 Front St. E. (Jarvis St.) | 416-365-3649
www.springrolls.ca

Whether it's "Viet, Chinese or Thai", something on the "diverse menu" is "bound to tempt you" at this "friendly", unusually "stylish" Pan-Asian quartet; fans feel the "quick, tasty" eats at "satisfyingly low prices" evince "consistent quality from location to location" – consequently, these chain links are "good places to get together with friends."

Starfish Oyster Bed & Grill ☒ *Seafood*   26 | 19 | 22 | $70

St. Lawrence | 100 Adelaide St. E. (bet. Church & Jarvis Sts.) |
416-366-7827 | www.starfishoysterbed.com

Everyone knows "great things come in small packages", and that goes for the "exceptional" bivalves at this St. Lawrence seafooder (owned by World Oyster Opening Champion Patrick McMurray) as well as the "memorable" pleasures to be found within its "cosy", "understated" confines; for a "lesson" in freshness, "sit at the bar" and chat with "knowledgeable" shuckers over a mug of microbrewed stout.

Studio Cafe *Italian/Mediterranean*   22 | 22 | 23 | $63

Bloor Yorkville | Four Seasons Hotel | 21 Avenue Rd. (Bloor St. W.) |
416-928-7330 | www.fourseasons.com/toronto

"Drop in anytime" to this "casual" but "pricey" cafe at the Four Seasons for some "Bloor Yorkville people-watching", a "power breakfast" or a "business lunch"; the "imaginative" Italian-Med eats are "presented well" by a "polished" crew, so while a few find the "art-filled" room "a bit cold", devotees declare there's "no better way to spend a Saturday."

	FOOD	DECOR	SERVICE	COST

Sultan's Tent *French/Moroccan* | 20 | 25 | 18 | $53

St. Lawrence | 49 Front St. E. (Church St.) | 416-961-0601 |
www.thesultanstent.com

You're actually in St. Lawrence, but the "intimate" tented rooms, arched doorways and tropical palms at this French-Moroccan "make you feel like you're in Marrakesh"; an "excellent variety" of "tasty" regional specialties ensures it's "fun for a large party", especially as nightly belly dancing shows ramp up the "exotic feel"; still, some say service can tend toward "Mediterranean casual."

Supermarket ⑧ *Asian Fusion* | ▽ 21 | 15 | 17 | $34

Chinatown-Kensington | 268 Augusta Ave. (College St.) | 416-840-0501 |
www.supermarkettoronto.com

Mini-Market *Asian Fusion*

NEW **Little Italy** | 596 College St. (Clinton St.) | 416-531-2822 |
www.tempotoronto.com

A "grunge nightclub posing as a restaurant", this Chinatown-Kensington "hipster hangout" has an "irreverently entertaining staff" serving up its "creative and tasty" Asian fusion "tapas-style menu"; "go with friends" to enjoy seasonal wine lists, a 30-seat patio and live music; N.B. the Little Italy location serves the same eats in a more intimate setting.

⊠ Sushi Kaji Ⓜ *Japanese* | 29 | 19 | 25 | $122

Mimico | 860 The Queensway (Islington Ave.) | 416-252-2166 |
www.sushikaji.com

"Don't let your first impressions cloud your judgment" – this "unassuming" 30-seat Mimico Japanese, voted Toronto's No. 1 for Food, is a "hidden treasure"; with "talent and a wry sense of humour", "artist" Mitsuhiro Kaji creates "sumptuous sashimi and sublime sushi" from sea creatures who "move from packing crate to dinner plate in seconds" ("fish so fresh it really does flop around"), while his "intriguing and expertly presented" omakase incorporates "exquisite hot dishes" as well; N.B. prix fixe only.

Sushi on Bloor *Japanese* | 20 | 11 | 15 | $24

Annex | 515 Bloor St. W. (Bathurst St.) | 416-516-3456 |
www.sushionbloor.com

"Loud, crowded" and "casual", this "affordable" Annex Japanese is a "student hangout" whose regulars report "excellent value throughout the menu" (e.g. rolls featuring "great combos", house-specialty sushi pizza); "so-so service" and "no ambience" don't deter devotees content to wait in "obscenely long line-ups."

Z Susur ☒Ⓜ *Asian Fusion/French*　　27 | 24 | 24 | $120

King West | 601 King St. W. (Bathurst St.) | 416-603-2205 | www.susur.com
"Adventurous foodies" make their way to King West for Susur Lee's "cutting-edge", "complex", "diverse yet cohesive" French-inflected Asian fusion fare (especially "brilliant" tasting menus in which "mains come first"); "gracious" staffers are "informative" and "minimalist decor" with "spaceship lighting" is "ultrahip" to boot – but be sure to "call your financial planner" and set aside "at least four hours" for dinner; still, a vocal minority is "not too sure about Susur", deeming its "shock-therapy approach" to cuisine "highly overrated."

Swan *Eclectic*　　24 | 19 | 21 | $42

Queen West Gallery District | 892 Queen St. W. (Strachan Ave.) | 416-532-0452
"Warm, convivial" and "quaint", this "upscale diner" in the Queen West Gallery District is "a perfect retro package" where "sublime" Eclectic fare ("addictive short ribs", "spanking fresh oysters" and perhaps the street's "best brunch") comes courtesy of "quick and friendly" servers; consequently, with only 30 seats, it's no wonder this "perennial favourite" is "always packed."

Swatow ●♥ *Chinese*　　21 | 5 | 15 | $21

Chinatown-Kensington | 309 Spadina Ave. (Dundas St. W.) | 416-977-0601
Party people pop into this cash-only Chinatown joint "post-club" for "huge portions" of "cheap" "late-night comfort food" of the Cantonese and Szechuan varieties, served "remarkably fast"; there's "no decor per se" ("bright white lights make you think you're about to undergo surgery"), but the chow "makes up for it."

Tabülè *Mideastern*　　▽ 25 | 16 | 22 | $36

Midtown | 2009 Yonge St. (Belsize Dr.) | 416-483-3747 | www.tabule.ca
"Superb", "wonderfully fresh" Middle Eastern eats (especially the "namesake" dish) purveyed by "friendly, helpful" servers draw crowds to this "cheerful", contemporary Midtowner; unfortunately, the 48-seat spot's "success" has resulted in "line-ups out the door."

	FOOD	DECOR	SERVICE	COST

Terra *Eclectic*

| 25 | 20 | 23 | $87 |

Thornhill | 8199 Yonge St. (Hwy. 407) | 905-731-6161 |
www.terrarestaurant.ca

For "downtown quality (and prices) in suburbia", this "upscale" Thornhill Eclectic is a "true gem" say surveyors who swoon over "fabulous" small plates – also found at the tapas and oyster-bar lounge – and a "thoughtful" California-heavy wine list; given a "knowledgeable staff", it all adds up to a "worthwhile treat for a special occasion."

☑ Terroni *Italian/Pizza*

| 22 | 16 | 16 | $34 |

Downtown Core | 106 Victoria St. (south of Queen St. E.) | 416-955-0258 ⑤
Midtown | 1 Balmoral Ave. (Yonge St.) | 416-925-4020
Queen West West | 720 Queen St. W. (Bathurst St.) | 416-504-0320
www.terroni.ca

"Fresh and inventive" thin-crust pizzas are "the glory of the house" at this "kinetic", "family-oriented" Southern Italian trio; though service from the "hip young" staff is "brisk at best" and often "erratic", cognoscenti claim the chainlet provides "great value for the dollar", which explains why it's "always packed."

Tomi-Kro ⑤ Ⓜ *Eclectic*

| ▽ 21 | 19 | 22 | $52 |

Leslieville | 1214 Queen St. E. (Leslie St.) | 416-463-6677

At this Leslieville Eclectic, the "affable" "staff and kitchen have the best of intentions", as manifested in "extremely tasty" eats complemented by a "deep wine list"; a recently expanded boho space (including a bar area) helps to foster an "ultrahip" vibe that draws in "late-night locals."

Tom Jones Steak House ❶ *Steak*

| 21 | 15 | 21 | $77 |

St. Lawrence | 17 Leader Ln. (bet. Church & Yonge Sts.) | 416-366-6583 |
www.tomjonessteakhouse.com

It's not unusual for surveyors to love this 40-year-old St. Lawrence reef 'n' beefer, what with its "awesome steaks", 700-label wine cellar and staffers who "do everything to please"; though the "throwback" setting "won't impress the modernist", some say it's "so old-school it's cool."

NEW Torito ⑤ *Spanish*

| - | - | - | M |

Chinatown-Kensington | Kensington Mkt. | 276 Augusta Ave.
(bet. College & Oxford Sts.) | 647-436-5874

Its name may translate to 'little bull', but this Kensington newcomer conjures up big flavours with its menu of authentic Spanish tapas accented with South and Central American flourishes and paired with a solid wine list; simple wooden tables and bullfight posters add to the relaxed ambience, while a no-reservations policy means you may encounter a line-up; N.B. dinner-only.

Toulà Ristorante & Bar *Italian*   16 | 20 | 19 | $71
Harbourfront | Westin Harbour Castle Hotel | 1 Harbour Sq., 38th fl. (bet. Bay & York Sts.) | 416-777-2002 | www.toularestaurant.com
With "captivating" 360-degree views from the 38th floor of the Westin Harbour Castle Hotel, this Harbourfront Northern Italian will "impress the eye" but "perhaps not so much the stomach"; respondents call the "authentic" cuisine "unmemorable" and "overpriced", but say they often bring "out-of-town guests" nonetheless.

Trapper's *Canadian/Continental*   20 | 17 | 21 | $79
North Toronto | 3479 Yonge St. (Lawrence Ave.) | 416-482-6211 | www.trappersrestaurant.ca
Spotlighting ingredients from across the country (salmon, mussels, maple syrup), this "welcoming" "North Toronto institution" proffers a "straightforward menu" of Canadian-Continental cookery; voters are split on the "classic" food ("reliable" vs. "predictable"), but almost all agree the "tired" interior could use a redo.

Trattoria Fieramosca *Italian*   19 | 18 | 20 | $51
Annex | 36A Prince Arthur Ave. (Bedford Rd.) | 416-323-0636 | www.fieramoscatoronto.com
"Courteous" people attract *amici* to this "casual" Annex Southern Italian offering "traditional" (read: "heavy" and "hearty") eats along with 35 wines by the glass; though comrades call it a "quaint, warm" place to "spend an evening", others dis "unexciting food" and "faded" digs; N.B. a spring 2007 renovation may outdate the above Decor score.

Trattoria Giancarlo ⊠ *Italian*   24 | 18 | 21 | $72
Little Italy | 41 Clinton St. (College St.) | 416-533-9619
Serving up "always fabulous", "authentic" *cucina* in Little Italy – "a rarity these days", ironically – plus an "extensive", "expensive" wine list, this "sophisticated" yet "comfy" trattoria is a "Toronto institution", with a "helpful" staff that's "neither pretentious nor absent"; you can escape the "din" in the "small" exposed-brick dining room by opting for a seat on the "amazing patio."

	FOOD	DECOR	SERVICE	COST

NEW trevor kitchen & bar 🅂 Ⓜ *Canadian* | – | – | – | E |

Downtown Core | 38 Wellington St. E. (bet. Church & Yonge Sts.) |
416-941-9410 | www.trevorkitchenandbar.com

Tucked below street level, this cosy Downtown Core Canadian from
chef-owner Trevor Wilkinson specializes in creative comfort fare; while
foodies will appreciate the chef's table, everyone else will be more than
satisfied dining amid the 150-year-old building's original architecture;
N.B. the intimate ambience extends to a candlelit bar with two lounges.

🄩 Truffles 🅂 *French* | 26 | 26 | 26 | $97 |

Bloor Yorkville | Four Seasons Hotel | 21 Avenue Rd. (Bloor St. W.) |
416-928-7331 | www.fourseasons.com/toronto

"They don't trifle" at this "exceptional" New French, a "gourmand's
delight" in Bloor Yorkville's Four Seasons, where the "delectable", almost "flawless" dishes are "adeptly paired with appropriate wines"
from a "superb" list; what with the staff's "courtesy" and "attention to
detail", diners love to "linger for hours" in the "intimate" room.

Tulip *Steak* | 19 | 8 | 16 | $29 |

Leslieville | 1606 Queen St. E. (Coxwell Ave.) | 416-469-5797 |
www.tulipsteakhouse.com

At this "reliable, cheap" and "always busy" Leslieville "landmark",
open since 1949, "high-end steaks at low-down prices" are served in
"hearty portions" ("wear your stretchy pants"); there's "no attitude"
and "no b.s." here, so expect a "step-above-a-greasy-spoon" setting.

Tutti Matti 🅂 *Italian* | 22 | 17 | 20 | $52 |

Entertainment District | 364 Adelaide St. W. (Spadina Ave.) | 416-597-8839 |
www.tuttimatti.com

At this Entertainment District eatery, chef-owner Alida Solomon
shows off her "passion" via "amazing homemade pasta" and other
"fresh", "authentic" Tuscan cuisine, matched with wines of the same
region; it may be "pricey", but earth-toned cafe-style decor and highly
rated service make this place a "nice little discovery."

Universal Grill Ⓜ *Eclectic* | 20 | 13 | 17 | $44 |

Hillcrest-Davenport | 1071 Shaw St. (Dupont St.) | 416-588-5928 |
www.universalgrill.ca

"Escape a dreary winter's night" with the "tasty" eats at this "funky",
"cosy" Hillcrest-Davenport Eclectic where "reclaimed drugstore-soda-

fountain" aesthetics create the "campy feel of a diner gone lounge"; though some deem it "inexpensive", others opine "prices will surprise you – in a not-so-good way."

Vertical 🗷 *Italian*

–	–	–	E

Financial District | First Canadian Pl. | 100 King St. W. (bet. Bay & York Sts.) | 416-214-2252 | www.verticalrestaurant.ca

With its seasonal Southern Italian menu, expansive wine list and convenient Financial District location, it's no surprise this upscale restaurant draws an expense-account crowd; but while elegant touches like Riedel stemware and wine lockers up the ante here, a mezzanine patio with a waterfall view makes this a relaxing option for non-business types too; N.B. open for lunch and dinner Monday–Friday.

Xacutti *Indian*

25	23	20	$70

Little Italy | 503 College St. (Palmerston Ave.) | 416-323-3957 | www.xacutti.com

"Scenesters" swarm this "chichi" "modern" Indian (pronounced 'sha-koo-tee') in Little Italy for its "innovative", "funked-up" and "delicious twists" on traditional entrees (plus desserts "worth loosening your belt for"); as a result, it's often "hard to get a table", and some say servers can be "snooty."

Zee Grill 🗷 *Seafood*

▽ 23	18	20	$66

Midtown | 641 Mt. Pleasant Rd. (bet. Davisville & Eglinton Aves.) | 416-484-6428 | www.zeegrill.com

Pescavores get a different kind of raw deal at this Midtown seafooder featuring "amazing oysters" and shellfish from on-site tanks; the venue has a "warm" "neighbourhood feel" fostered by "friendly" staffers, which may be why cronies confide it's an "ideal spot to sneak away to for an evening."

Zucca Trattoria *Italian*

24	19	23	$61

Midtown | 2150 Yonge St. (south of Eglinton Ave.) | 416-488-5774 | www.zuccatrattoria.com

This "upscale" Midtown Italian pleases with "authentic", "market- and season-centred" cookery "with real flair" ("excellent fresh fish", homemade pasta) bolstered by a "reasonable wine list"; thanks to the "charming" crew that populates the "comfortable" premises, *amici* aver it's "like eating at a friend's house."

RESTAURANTS

	FOOD	DECOR	SERVICE	COST

Outlying Areas

Eigensinn Farm Ⓜ⇄ *French*   29 | 19 | 27 | $166

Singhampton | Rural Rd. 2 (20 km. south of Collingwood) | 519-922-3128

At his "intimate" Singhampton farmhouse some 160 km (100 miles) northwest of Toronto, Michael Stadtländer conjures up "magical", "exquisite" French cuisine from his own "extraordinarily fresh" organic ingredients ("that lamb on your plate was frolicking in the field yesterday"); "serious culinarians" swear "it's worth the drive and cost" – just remember to "bring your own wine"; N.B. hours are seasonal.

Inn on the Twenty *Canadian*   23 | 25 | 22 | $78

Jordan | Inn on the Twenty | 3836 Main St. (Hwy. 8/King St.) | 905-562-7313 | www.innonthetwenty.com

"Overlooking wine country" and nearby 20-Mile Creek, this Niagara Region inn augments a "stunning" vista with "inventive" Canadian cuisine proffered by an "attentive" staff; though critics claim the "expensive" fare "has faded a bit", this is "great for Sunday brunch", especially if you're "visiting the shops in Jordan Village."

Peller Estates Winery Restaurant *Continental*   26 | 24 | 24 | $77

Niagara-on-the-Lake | Peller Estates Winery | 290 John St. E. (Niagara Pkwy.) | 905-468-4678 | www.peller.com

The "serene" landscape alone makes the experience "gratifying" – but there's a big "bonus" at this Niagara-on-the-Lake "château" winery/dinery: "creative" Continental cuisine crafted from "fresh local ingredients" ("go with the tasting menu"); "solicitious" staffers deliver "exemplary service" in the "elegant yet unpretentious" Gallic-inflected interior.

Vineland Estates Ⓜ *Canadian*   26 | 26 | 24 | $76

Vineland | 3620 Moyer Rd. (Victoria Ave.) | 905-562-7088 | www.vineland.com

"Spectacular views" from the patio at this Niagara Region winery make diners "feel [they're] in seventh heaven" – or "in Tuscany" – as they sip house vintages and sup on "superb", locally sourced Canadian cuisine (a recent chef change may outdate the above Food score); "lunch is the bargain" here, but given "exceptional" service, even the $100 five-course dinner with pairings is "a great value"; N.B. it's closed Mondays and Tuesdays in winter.

NIGHTLIFE
DIRECTORY

Nightlife

Ratings & Symbols

Appeal, **Decor** and **Service** are rated on a 0 to 30 scale.

Cost reflects surveyors' estimated price (in Canadian dollars) of a typical single drink. For places listed without ratings, the price range is:

⌐I⌐ below $5   ⌐E⌐ $9 to $11
⌐M⌐ $5 to $8   ⌐VE⌐ more than $11

MOST POPULAR	TOP APPEAL
1. Drake, The	24 Ultra Supper Club
2. Roof Lounge	Roof Lounge
3. Panorama	Second City
4. Yuk Yuks	23 Woody's/Sailor
5. Ultra Supper Club	Drake, The

Andy Poolhall
21 | 19 | 16 | $7

Little Italy | 489 College St. (Bathurst St.) | 416-923-5300 | www.andypoolhall.com

"Loud and groovy", with a "mix of things to do", this "retro" Little Italy lounge draws "young twentysomethings" seeking a "very cool" "place to chill" and "meet friends"; "really good DJs" plus live music keeps the "great dance floor" hopping, while the rhythmically challenged entertain themselves at five pool tables and a central bar; "overworked" staffers serve food till midnight and drinks till 2:45 AM daily.

Black Bull Hotel & Tavern
17 | 11 | 16 | $8

Queen West | 298 Queen St. W. (Soho St.) | 416-593-2766

"Perfect for what it is" – a "wild and wooly landmark" since 1833, where patrons "leave their pretensions at the door" – this "low-key", "dingy-ish" Queen West pub is known for having the "best see-and-be-seen patio around", a "strategically located" corner space ideal for a "quick bite" and "people-watching over a pint of beer"; N.B. the upstairs rooming house is for long-term boarders only.

APPEAL	DECOR	SERVICE	COST

Bovine Sex Club

18 | 17 | 14 | $11

Queen West | 542 Queen St. W. (Bathurst St.) | 416-504-4239 |
www.bovinesexclub.com

"Don't let the name scare you away" – bestiality is not on the agenda
at this "real-deal" Queen West club, the "underbelly of Toronto rock"
complete with "loud music" (including live bands), "lots of leather"
and "great Goth appeal"; the "trashy, fun" scene is always "full of characters" thanks to a "surprisingly relaxed and friendly atmosphere" and
theme nights that draw "a mixed crowd you won't find anywhere else."

Brant House

22 | 23 | 18 | $11

King West | 1 Brant St. (Spadina Ave.) | 416-703-2800 |
www.branthouse.com

"If you enjoy dancing and people-watching", this King West eatery and
lounge in a renovated 100-year-old warehouse is a "great place to do
both"; the clientele ranges from "geeky" boogie men to "porn stars" and
"all the hip cats in between", not to mention hordes of "young Bay Street
brokers"; since drinks tend toward the "overpriced", respondents recommend going with friends and "splurging on [a bottle] service" table.

Century Room

20 | 22 | 17 | $12

King West | 580 King St. W. (Portland St.) | 416-203-2226 |
www.centuryroom.com

This sleek, "chic, fun and enjoyable" club in trendy King West draws
hip Downtowners three nights a week with "great music" and "big
dance floors"; those who find the "expensive" tariffs "worth it" report
it's also a "nice place to hang out" if you opt for a private booth with bot-
tle service or an alfresco interlude on the tree-lined patio; N.B. open
Tuesdays, Fridays and Saturdays till 2 AM.

C Lounge

20 | 25 | 14 | $10

Entertainment District | 456 Wellington St. W. (bet. Portland St. &
Spadina Ave.) | 416-260-9393 | www.libertygroup.com

Seasonal switcheroos ("hot patio/pool area" with umbrellas in the
summer, "ice bar in the winter") and servers in "sexy uniforms" spice up
this Entertainment District showplace where "dolled-up" women "jiggle
to Top 40 tunes" on the dance floor, then retire to spacious bathrooms
offering massage and makeup application; it has "snooty" doormen
and it's "expensive", but the experience is "worth every penny."

	APPEAL	DECOR	SERVICE	COST

Docks

17	13	14	$11

Port of Toronto | 11 Polson St. (Cherry St.) | 416-469-5655 |
www.thedocks.com

Various "diversions" entice Torontonians to this "multifaceted entertainment complex" at the port, such as "all-ages concerts", a rooftop bar
with "breathtaking views of the city at night", soccer and golf areas,
drive-in movies and a pool; proponents praise summer's "South Beach
Sundays" and find the club nights "chic and fun", but critics condemn the
place as "anonymous", "phony", "overpriced" and "out of the way."

☑ Drake, The
(Lounge, Underground, Sky Yard)

23	23	18	$10

Queen West Gallery District | The Drake Hotel | 1150 Queen St. W.
(Beaconsfield Ave.) | 416-531-5042 | www.thedrakehotel.ca

"A little off the beaten track" in the Queen West Gallery District, this
"trendy" trio in the Drake Hotel draws an "arty, intellectual crowd"
that appreciates its "eclectic vibe"; the basement features live music
nightly, the street-level section combines "excellent DJs", a burnished
bronze bar and a "cosy", "loungey atmosphere", and the "exceptional"
Moroccan-inflected rooftop boasts "couches, a huge movie screen"
and, on occasion, "boundary-stretching" performance art.

El Convento Rico

-	-	-	M

Little Italy | 750 College St. (bet. Crawford & Shaw Sts.) | 416-588-7800 |
www.elconventorico.com

Early birds beware: things don't heat up until late at this Latin gay club,
but when the clock strikes 1 AM on Fridays and 12:30 AM on Saturdays,
get ready to watch the venue's deservedly famous drag show; a Little
Italy mainstay for just over 15 years, it welcomes everyone with its hot
salsa, moderately priced drinks and always crowded dance floor.

Fluid

-	-	-	M

Entertainment District | 217 Richmond St. W. (John St.) | 416-593-6116 |
www.fluidlounge.ca

Reopened after renovations, this decade-old clubland veteran in the
heart of the Entertainment District features dramatic new decor elements that include thousands of glass 'teardrops' dangling from the
ceiling; there are DJs spinning in its two rooms, and you can expect to
see plenty of beautiful people, especially on 'Sexy Back Saturdays.'

Guvernment/Kool Haus

			M
–	–	–	M

Downtown Core | 132 Queens Quay E. (Jarvis St.) | 416-869-0045 | www.theguvernment.com

Encompassing seven clubs on five floors with room for 4,000 people, it's no wonder this Downtown Core party palace is one of Toronto's main destinations for dancing, DJs and live music; while the Guvernment boasts state-of-the-art sound and lighting and the Kool Haus draws some of the top names in music, four other themed lounge spaces and a rooftop bar with city views prove there's something here for just about everyone.

Horseshoe Tavern

21	10	16	$7

Queen West | 370 Queen St. W. (Spadina Ave.) | 416-598-4753 | www.horseshoetavern.com

A "historic hole", this slightly "grungy" yet "bigger-than-life" Queen West "legend" (since 1947) is "a must-visit for live music fans", who cherish it as a "great" "place to catch up-and-coming acts" and "intimate concerts" that's still "large enough to be exciting"; "don't bother to dress up" – just "hunker down for some big-time beer swilling" at this "rockabilly heaven"; N.B. cover charge varies.

Live@Courthouse

			E
–	–	–	E

St. Lawrence | 57 Adelaide St. E. (bet. Church & Toronto Sts.) | 416-214-9379 | www.liveatcourthouse.com

Jazz aficionados get a new place to show the love with the opening of this swank live music venue located in a historic, high-ceilinged former courthouse near St. Lawrence Market; able to accommodate anything from trios to big bands, it showcases a wide variety of musical styles performed by local and touring acts; meanwhile, the kitchen serves light fare and there's also an intimate downstairs lounge with comfy couches and plasma-screen views of the stage.

N'Awlins

20	17	21	$11

Entertainment District | 299 King St. W. (John St.) | 416-595-1958 | www.nawlins.ca

For "great live jazz" head to this "cosy Cajun-themed" bar in the Entertainment District that's nowadays almost "more New Orleans than the real thing"; the "fun atmosphere" at this "intimate" spot makes it suitable "for a date or hanging out with friends", while a food menu (served till at least 11 PM) and "really nice specialty martinis" help keep the good times rolling.

⚡ Panorama   23 | 22 | 16 | $12

Bloor Yorkville | Manulife Ctr. | 55 Bloor St. W., 51st fl. (Bay St.) | 416-967-0000 | www.panoramalounge.com

True to its name, this "romantic", "stylish" Bloor Yorkville bar "perched on the 51st floor of the Manulife Centre" provides expansive skyline vistas from the city's highest outdoor patio, plus an interior done up in Bauhaus style; drinks are "pricey" and there is a "$5 cover on weekends", but for an "intimate first date", the "breathtaking ambience" is "worth paying for."

Republik   21 | 21 | 20 | $12

Entertainment District | 261 Richmond St. W. (John St.) | 416-598-1632 | www.republiknightclub.com

Republikans "dance, dance, dance the night away" at this 16,000-sq.-ft. party space in the Entertainment District, rocking out in the main room with dizzying colour strobes and laser lights, rotating plasma screens and a skull-vibrating 200,000 watts of sound (sometimes provided by DJ, other times by live acts); though it's "large enough that the pickings are good", surveyors say privacy lovers can still find "quiet spots" to enjoy "more intimate moments."

Revival   22 | 20 | 17 | $9

Little Italy | 783 College St. W. (Shaw St.) | 416-535-7888 | www.revivalbar.com

Located in a "converted church" with a "long-standing good vibe", this Little Italy club exalts its faithful with "great indie bands" ("go during the week" and "get your groove on"), popular theme nights ("mod night is awesome") and "lots of beautiful people"; believers preach "go in with a healthy sense of humour" and "the music will keep you happy all night", but doubters dislike "jostling" ("no traffic flow in this bar") and debatable acoustics.

Rivoli Pool Hall   18 | 15 | 18 | $9

Queen West | 334 Queen St. W. (Spadina Ave.) | 416-596-1501 | www.rivoli.ca

Part of a Queen West restaurant/bar/club complex that "appeals to all different types", this "laid-back" "institution" is a "standard local haunt"; the "great" upstairs pool venue and lounge offers 11 tables plus video games and, on alternate Sundays, karaoke; the decor "leaves much to be desired", but at least you "can order munchies" till midnight.

☑ Roof Lounge
24 | 21 | 23 | $15

Bloor Yorkville | Park Hyatt Toronto | 4 Avenue Rd., 18th fl. (Bloor St.) | 416-324-1568 | www.parktoronto.hyatt.com

"The ultimate urban oasis" is this "comfortable, old-school" bar perched on the 18th floor of Bloor Yorkville's Park Hyatt Toronto; it offers "great views" of Downtown and the lake plus "quality service" from "authentic bartenders", so it's "fabulous" for a leisurely drink, whether by the "roaring wood fireplace" that lends the room a "warm" glow or on the "lovely" seasonal terrace; N.B. food served till 1 AM.

Rosewater Supper Club
20 | 22 | 16 | $13

St. Lawrence | 19 Toronto St. (bet. Adelaide & King Sts.) | 416-214-5888 | www.libertygroup.com

This "jewel" set in a landmark St. Lawrence building boasts 22-ft. ceilings and hardwood and marble floors that give the "beautiful room" a "classy feel"; jazz performances Thursdays and Saturdays attract "sizable crowds", and though some deem it "more restaurant than nightspot" (food served till 11 PM), it's nonetheless an "elegant" destination.

☑ Second City
24 | 16 | 18 | $14

Entertainment District | 51 Mercer St. (Blue Jays Way) | 416-343-0011 | www.secondcity.com

"Always good for a laugh", this recently relocated branch of the "comedy club that launched a million careers" (e.g. Dan Aykroyd, Martin Short, John Candy, Mike Myers) is still an Entertainment District "classic"; in fact, you may even find "future *Saturday Night Live* stars" doing standup, improv or sketches on the venue's small stage.

Social, The
22 | 16 | 16 | $9

Queen West Gallery District | 1100 Queen St. W. (Dovercourt Rd.) | 416-532-4474 | www.thesocial.ca

"Good old rock", "funkalicious beats" from the '80s and '90s and local indie bands keep Socialites grooving at this "retro", comparatively "unpretentious" Queen West Gallery District bar; it's "the latest hot spot" for "hipsters", thanks in no small part to the "coolest" atmosphere, affordable drinks and "no cover."

	APPEAL	DECOR	SERVICE	COST

⚡ Ultra Supper Club
APPEAL 24 | DECOR 25 | SERVICE 18 | COST $13

Queen West | 314 Queen St. W. (Peter St.) | 416-263-0330 |
www.ultrasupperclub.com

Decorated with a "gorgeous" "mix of Moroccan" and "Indonesian-type" elements filtered through a "funky" "industrial-lounge" aesthetic, this "sexy, sophisticated spot" in Queen West is "the place to see and be seen" according to a "hip yet mature clientele" that comes for "fine food and wine", then "hangs around to dance" or sip drinks on the "beautiful" rooftop patio; an "obscure" entrance behind a set of doors and down a path "makes it that much more intriguing."

Wheat Sheaf
APPEAL 16 | DECOR 9 | SERVICE 18 | COST $6

King West | 667 King St. W. (Bathurst St.) | 416-504-9912

"Toronto's first pub" (founded 1849) happens to be situated in über-trendy King West, but this "local watering hole" is undoubtedly "old-school"; it's "a place to kick back with the boys, play some pool", down some "moderately priced brewskis and above-average pub fare", and share a "good laugh" – plus, there's no need to "wear your best duds."

⚡ Woody's/Sailor
APPEAL 23 | DECOR 18 | SERVICE 19 | COST $9

Church & Wellesley | 465-467 Church St. (north of Carlton St.) |
416-972-0887

Known for "hot bartenders" and an "extremely attractive" crowd, this "entertaining and friendly" watering hole in the Church and Wellesley gay village is "still a great place for men to meet men"; as "a bar, not a club", it's "a lot more relaxed", yet there's "always something going on" (nightly DJs, theme parties, house-sponsored amateur sports teams); the adjacent Sailor boasts the same vibe in a nautical setting.

⚡ Yuk Yuks Downtown
APPEAL 21 | DECOR 13 | SERVICE 16 | COST $13

Entertainment District | 224 Richmond St. W. (bet. Duncan & Simcoe Sts.) |
416-967-6425 | www.yukyuks.com

"The place to go" for a "hilarious night out with friends", this Entertainment District outpost of the Canadian "comedy chain" is a "crowded, dark" den where pro comics whip up "interactive" fun with the "packed-in" audience (Tuesday is Amateur Night); "expect typical bar food, premium-priced drinks" and "spotty service", but if the "raunchy jokes" are on target, it's "a hit" nevertheless; N.B. cover charge varies depending on the day.

ATTRACTIONS DIRECTORY

Attractions

Ratings & Symbols

Appeal, Facilities and **Service** are rated on a 0 to 30 scale.

Cost reflects the attraction's high-season price range (in Canadian dollars) for one adult:

$0 Free
I $10 or less
M $11–$25

E $26–$40
VE $41 or more

MOST POPULAR
1. CN Tower
2. Ontario Science Centre
3. Toronto Zoo
4. Hockey Hall of Fame
5. Royal Ontario Museum

TOP APPEAL
26 Hockey Hall of Fame
Toronto Islands
Ontario Science Centre
Toronto Zoo
25 Royal Ontario Museum

Air Canada Centre
22 | 23 | 18 | E

Entertainment District | 40 Bay St. (Lakeshore Blvd.) | 416-815-5500 | www.theaircanadacentre.com

The city's "premier venue" for sporting and music events is this "modern", "convenient" Entertainment District arena with a capacity of almost 20,000; among its charms are "clear" sight lines "from even the highest level" and an on-site brewery that "adds character", so though ticket prices may be "too much for some country bumpkins", the majority of surveyors agree there's "no better place to catch a hockey game."

Allan Gardens Conservatory
20 | 18 | 16 | $0

Cabbagetown | 19 Horticultural Ave. (Gerrard St.) | 416-392-7288 | www.toronto.ca

Quite literally an "oasis", this "beautiful", "charming" Victorian conservatory in an "iffy" section of Cabbagetown features six greenhouses in which "tropical flora stand next to a wing of dry succulents"; during "the monotony of a long winter", a stroll through (with or without a tour guide) evokes a much-needed "vacation in an exotic land" –

but "avoid Saturdays" during wedding season, as "every bride in Toronto gets her photos taken here."

Art Gallery of Ontario
`25` `23` `20` `I`

Grange Park | 317 Dundas St. W. (McCaul St.) | 416-979-6648 | www.ago.net
For "a day full of beauty and peace" aesthetes adore this "fabulous" repository in Grange Park, "one of those museums that can make anyone comfortable" as they enjoy the "fine collections" ("fantastic Henry Moore sculptures"), "terrific lectures" and "awesome gift shop"; renovations through 2008 will "re-dress the gallery" in a design by Toronto-born architect Frank Gehry; N.B. closed Mondays and Tuesdays.

Bata Shoe Museum
`22` `22` `20` `I`

Annex | 327 Bloor St. W. (St. George St.) | 416-979-7799 | www.batashoemuseum.ca
"Heaven on earth for Imelda Marcos-wannabes", this "whimsical" museum set in a "striking, contemporary" Annex edifice houses more than 14,000 "fascinating" pieces of "footwear history" (e.g. cultural analysis as well as artifacts from celebs like Marilyn Monroe and Elvis Presley); "shoe fetishists rejoice", of course, but even those not usually "dazzled" by such things confess it's "strange yet enrapturing" – "a shoo-in."

Beach, The
`25` `17` `16` `$0`

The Beach | Queen St. E., from Neville Park Blvd. to Woodbine Ave.
Toronto may be a "cold northern town", but this "funky, upscale" lakefront district has "a laid-back Southern California feel" with its "miles of boardwalk" and trail for blading and biking, "beach volleyball everywhere" and "parks for the kids"; "eclectic restaurants and shops" dot the area, but it's also "a beautiful spot to relax, unwind" and "mingle with Torontonians"; P.S. "don't miss July's annual jazz festival."

Black Creek Pioneer Village
`-` `-` `-` `M`

North Toronto | 1000 Murray Ross Pkwy. (Steeles Ave.) | 416-736-1733 | www.blackcreek.ca
Take a trip back in time at this collection of restored 19th-century homes, shops and gardens in North Toronto, where families can visit a cider mill, piggery or one-room schoolhouse, watch costumed artisans demonstrate skills like blacksmithing and take their midday meal at the Halfway House Inn & Restaurant; a hands-on Discovery Centre is an added bonus for the kids; N.B. open May 1–December 31.

ATTRACTIONS

	APPEAL	FACIL.	SERVICE	COST

Casa Loma
23 | 20 | 19 | M

Casa Loma | 1 Austin Terr. (Spadina Rd.) | 416-923-1171 | www.casaloma.org
"The former home of Sir Henry and Lady Pellatt", this "romantic" "urban castle" is now a "Toronto treasure" boasting a "secret underground tunnel", "sumptuous gardens" and "palatial stables"; "views of Downtown" make climbing the "winding" stairs to the turrets worthwhile, and the estate as a whole is "especially stunning" when "decorated for the [winter] holidays"; P.S. the fee includes an "informative" audio tour.

⊠ CN Tower
25 | 21 | 18 | E

Entertainment District | 301 Front St. W. (Bremner Blvd.) | 416-868-6937 | 888-684-3268 | www.cntower.ca
"You can't miss it, literally" – the "world's tallest freestanding structure" (553 m), located in the Entertainment District, is a "must-see" for "unparalleled" vistas from a "terrifying" "glass-floored" observation deck as well as educational exhibits and a "greatly improved" revolving restaurant ("grab a meal and get more value" for your admission fee); expect "long waits" and an "expensive elevator ride", but if you "go just before sunset", "you'll be stunned."

Design Exchange
∇ 19 | 15 | 15 | I

(aka DX)

Financial District | Toronto Dominion Ctr. | 234 Bay St. (King St.) | 416-363-6121 | www.dx.org
Housed in the erstwhile stock exchange building "smack in the middle" of the Financial District is this exhibit space intended to educate visitors on the value of design (industrial, graphic, architectural and otherwise); its "amazingly large ballroom – the former trading floor" – is the site of conferences, lectures and seminars, while the third level houses a permanent collection of Canadian design artifacts.

Distillery District
24 | 21 | 18 | $0

Distillery District | 55 Mill St. (Parliament St.) | 416-364-1177 | www.thedistillerydistrict.com
Once the British Empire's largest distillery, this "revitalized" 13-acre area with cobblestone streets and "beautiful old brick" structures feels like "a throwback to the 19th century"; "cute restaurants" and "quaint" shops may be "a little too chichi" for some ("take a few million dollars and enjoy the art galleries"), but farmer's markets, "imag-

inative" festivals and a "secret skating rink" provide visitors with more egalitarian "street entertainment."

Eaton Centre
20 | 21 | 17 | $0

Downtown Core | 220 Yonge St. (bet. Dundas & Queen Sts.) | 416-598-8700 | www.torontoeatoncentre.com

Built in 1977, this "one-stop shopping" complex in the Downtown Core is a "bustling" place perfect for "people-watching"; the tenants are mostly "typical" "chain stores" – "from budget-conscious to bling-bling" – but the "glass roof", "flying geese display" and sheer size (two city blocks) help to make this a "nice mid-afternoon diversion."

Elgin & Winter Garden Theatre Centre
23 | 22 | 19 | I

Downtown Core | 189 Yonge St. (Queen St.) | 416-325-4144 | www.heritagefdn.on.ca

It's "worth catching a show" at this double-decker pair of "whimsical", "ornate" vintage theatres in the Downtown Core, "magical spaces from a bygone age" that now feature plays, screenings, concerts and operas; you can also take "a trip back to vaudeville" via 90-minute backstage tours on Thursdays and Saturdays.

Harbourfront Centre
21 | 20 | 18 | $0

Harbourfront | 235 Queens Quay W. (Lower Simcoe St.) | 416-973-4000 | www.harbourfrontcentre.com

There's "a different festival each weekend" in the summer and "lots to do year-round" (over 4,000 events annually, including dance, theatre and the visual arts) at this "clean and classy" lakefront development; plus, "nonstop" "multiethnic" activities – from ice skating and "free music" to the renowned Harbourfront Reading Series – allow aesthetes to "experience the world in one place."

Z Hockey Hall of Fame
26 | 24 | 21 | M

Downtown Core | BCE Pl. | 30 Yonge St. (Front St.) | 416-360-7765 | www.hhof.com

Set in an "imposing old bank building" in the Downtown Core, this "hockey fanatic's dream" offers "comprehensive", "interactive displays" and "video simulators" ("pretend to be Mario, Wayne or Bobby") plus "cool authentic memorabilia" (e.g. Lord Stanley's "original cup", stored in what was once the bank's vault); the only quibble: loyal Canadiens fans grumble this "shrine" "should be in Montréal."

ATTRACTIONS

	APPEAL	FACIL.	SERVICE	COST

India Bazaar

| 18 | 10 | 13 | $0 |

India Bazaar | Gerrard St. E. (bet. Coxwell & Greenwood Aves.) | 416-465-8513 | www.gerrardindiabazaar.com

Toronto's "diversity" is on display at this "off-the-beaten-path" market district where "colourful saris" and the "aromas of betel nuts and curry" transport you to "another world"; aficionados advise "browse the shops" for Bollywood flicks, gold jewellery or subcontinental CDs, then enjoy "wonderful, inexpensive" South Indian cuisine "not found elsewhere in the city."

Kensington Market

| - | - | - | $0 |

Chinatown-Kensington | Bellevue Ave. to Dundas St. E.; College St. to Spadina Ave. | www.kensington-market.ca

The narrow streets of this vibrant, historic neighbourhood are packed with cafes, vendors, fishmongers, food shops and funky, trendy stores selling vintage furniture and clothing; from the globally sourced goods to the street musicians to the restaurants purveying eclectic eats, it all adds up to one of Toronto's most multicultural experiences.

Nathan Phillips Square

| 19 | 14 | 11 | $0 |

Downtown Core | 100 Queen St. W. (Bay St.) | 416-338-0338 | www.toronto.ca

Downtown's "once avant-garde" plaza in front of City Hall is a "romantic" place to "go skating in the winter" (a "free night out" if you "bring your [own] skates"), and summertime offers "interesting people-watching" thanks to "art shows, farmer's markets" and "free concerts"; if you're peckish, fries with gravy from the "chip trucks along Queen Street" are "a must."

Ontario Place

| 22 | 22 | 17 | M |

Harbourfront West | 955 Lakeshore Blvd. W. (Ontario Place Blvd.) | 416-314-9900 | 866-663-4386 | www.ontarioplace.com

Anchored on three man-made islands in Harbourfront West, this "lakeside amusement park" is a "great summer venue" for "kids and kids at heart"; it boasts "the original IMAX" and hosts "nighttime concerts", children's theatre and a July fireworks festival, plus pedal boats, heated waterslides and a marina; given that it's been open since 1971, however, some surveyors suggest the "outdated" facility may "need a face-lift."

APPEAL | FACIL. | SERVICE | COST

☑ Ontario Science Centre
26 | 25 | 21 | M

Don Mills | 770 Don Mills Rd. (Eglinton Ave.) | 416-696-1000 |
888-696-1110 | www.ontariosciencecentre.ca

An "all-day experience", this Don Mills science museum (founded in 1969) stimulates "kids, families and the geeks at heart"; most fans feel its time-tested, "imaginative", "hands-on" exhibits and "mind-blowing movie-theatre planetarium" are "well worth the price of admission", and the centre has added new indoor and outdoor displays as part of a recent $40 million "upgrade."

Rogers Centre
- | - | - | E

Downtown Core | 1 Blue Jays Way (bet. Front St. & Spadina Ave.) |
416 341-1707 | www.rogerscentre.com

Thanks to the world's first fully retractable stadium roof, you can watch a game or a concert under the open sky at this domed Downtown Core venue, the home of the Toronto Blue Jays and CFL Argonauts; one of the city's most recognizable landmarks, it boasts a behind-the-scenes tour that will take you to the dugouts, locker rooms and luxury suites; N.B. there are four restaurants that overlook the field.

☑ Royal Ontario Museum
25 | 23 | 21 | M

Bloor Yorkville | 100 Queen's Park (Bloor St.) | 416-586-8000 |
www.rom.on.ca

"Huge dinosaur skeletons", an "ancient Chinese tomb" and "unparalleled Egyptian artifacts" are to be found within the "world-class collections" at this Bloor Yorkville "maze" that specializes in international cultures and natural history; "ambitious" programs and a cafe feed mind and body, while architect Daniel Libeskind's new crystal-shaped addition (to be completed in June 2007) is proving an "eye-catching" extension; P.S. "go on Friday nights", when admission is only $5.

Steam Whistle Brewing
21 | 19 | 23 | I

Entertainment District | The Roundhouse | 255 Bremner Blvd.
(bet. Spadina Ave. & York St.) | 416-362-2337 | 866-240-2337 |
www.steamwhistle.ca

This "converted" "former train repair station" in the Entertainment District is an actual "working brewery" that lures hopsheads with "free samples" of its pilsner plus "root beer for the kids"; book one of their half-hour tours (offered daily) to watch "the process of making beer."

	APPEAL	FACIL.	SERVICE	COST

St. Lawrence Market Complex

| 24 | 18 | 21 | $0 |

St. Lawrence | 92 Front St. E. (Jarvis St.) | 416-392-7219 |
www.stlawrencemarket.com

A "must-see for foodies", this "old-fashioned" culinary bazaar is full of
"fantastic" meats, baked goods, fruits and vegetables, "eccentric
characters hawking their wares" and "steady crowds" that are "part of
the charm"; go on "Saturday early morning" (it opens at 5 AM) to enjoy
an "authentic" breakfast – regulars recommend Carousel Bakery's
"Canadian bacon on a bun" – and "fun" people-watching.

◪ Toronto Islands

| 26 | 19 | 18 | I |

Toronto Islands | 9 Queens Quay W. (Bay St.) | 416-392-8193 |
www.torontoharbour.com/toronto-islands

"Just a short ride from Downtown", this "tranquil" archipelago is an
"urban oasis" inviting day-trippers to "bring a picnic", "wander the
beaches", "rent boats or bikes" and visit the "small" amusement park
for children; while heading back to the "hustle and bustle", take in the
ferry's "scenic views" of the cityscape (they're "stunning at dusk") – or
extend your "escape" and stay in one of the "lovely" B&B cottages.

◪ Toronto Zoo

| 26 | 23 | 20 | M |

Scarborough | 361A Old Finch Ave. (Meadowvale Rd.) | 416-392-5900 |
www.torontozoo.com

"Bring your walking shoes", "pack a lunch" and "plan to spend a whole
day" at this mammoth menagerie in Scarborough where a "huge selection of animals" graze, growl and cavort "in natural-type enclosures";
it's a "bit out of the way", but once you get here, you'll find "excellent
facilities", including restaurants, camel rides, a virtual-reality habitat
and a water park; there's so much to do, veterans urge "take the shut-
tle" tour first to help you "decide where to spend your time."

Yonge-Dundas Square

| - | - | - | $0 |

Downtown Core | 1 Dundas St. E. (Yonge St.) | 416-979-9960 |
www.ydsquare.ca

Watch a movie under the stars, attend a free concert or check out the
vendors at this outdoor entertainment venue and public meeting space
in the heart of the Downtown Core; whether you're there to grab same-
day, half-price theatre tickets at the T.O. TIX booth or just resting your
legs, be sure to admire the interplay of the 20 computerized fountains.

HOTELS
DIRECTORY

Hotels

Ratings & Symbols

Rooms, Service, Dining and **Facilities** are rated on a 0 to 30 scale.

Cost reflects the hotel's high-season rate (in Canadian dollars) for a standard double room. It does not reflect seasonal changes.

👬 children's programs
✗ exceptional restaurant
⊕ historic interest
🍳 kitchens
🐾 allows pets
👀 views

⚲ 18-hole golf course
Ⓢ notable spa facilities
🎿 downhill skiing
🏊 swimming pools
🎾 tennis

Cosmopolitan Hotel & Spa 🍳👀Ⓢ

| – | – | – | – | $500 |

Downtown Core | 8 Colborne St. | 416-350-2000 | fax 350-2460 | 800-958-3488 | www.cosmotoronto.com | 95 suites, 2 penthouses

Merging Zen-like tranquility with boutique chic, this relatively new hotel tucked away on a small Downtown Core side street lives up to its sophisticated name; the suites (only five per floor) are designed with both feng shui and relaxation in mind: a burbling bamboo fountain and meditation mat share space with a kitchen, washer/dryer and flat-screen TV; the upscale vibe extends to the Japanese restaurant Doku 15 as well as the ultraluxe Shizen Spa.

Fairmont Royal York, The ⊕🐾👀Ⓢ🎿🏊

| 19 | 22 | 20 | 21 | $339 |

Financial District | 100 Front St. W. | 416-368-2511 | fax 368-9040 | 800-441-1414 | www.fairmont.com | 1174 rooms, 191 suites

For a "solid choice" in Downtown Toronto's Financial District, many turn to this "wonderful example of Fairmont hospitality", an "elegant", "ornate" 1843 "monument to Victorian style" where the "extremely helpful bellmen and concierge" win fans; while most reviewers applaud this railway hotel's "atmospheric public" areas and "old-world grace", skeptics say the "tired" "tiny" rooms "need remodelling."

HOTELS

	ROOMS	SERVICE	DINING	FACIL.	COST

Four Seasons ✗ 🅿 ⚲ 🏋 🌊 | 24 | 26 | 25 | 24 | $340 |

Bloor Yorkville | 21 Avenue Rd. | 416-964-0411 | fax 964-8699 |
800-332-3442 | www.fourseasons.com | 342 rooms, 38 suites
The "flawless" staff "fulfils all requests" at this "chic" Four Seasons
flagship "perfectly located in Yorkville" near Bloor Street; the "exceptional" dining at Truffles and an "amazing lobby bar" where you can
"hobnob with stars" are the standout features, but seasoned travelers
who believe this "old broad" is "showing her age" say the planned new
property nearby "will be a welcome replacement."

Hôtel Le Germain 👫 ✗ ⚲ | - | - | - | - | $495 |

Downtown Core | 30 Mercer St. | 416-345-9500 | fax 345-9501 |
866-345-9501 | www.germaintoronto.com | 118 rooms, 4 suites
Opened in 2003, this Downtown Core boutique hotel is known for its romantic ambience and dramatic design – the baths have windows looking
into the rooms, with blinds for privacy; even so, children's activities
make it an option for families too; special touches (like Aveda toiletries),
an upscale restaurant and a library lounge with fireplace up the ante.

Le Royal Méridien King Edward ⚲ 🏋 ⑤ | 21 | 22 | 19 | 19 | $425 |

St. Lawrence | 37 King St. E. | 416-863-3131 | fax 863-4102 | 800-543-4300 |
www.lemeridien.com | 248 rooms, 48 suites
"Pretend you're a royal relation" at this "refurbished landmark" in
St. Lawrence, "a bit of Edwardian splendour" known as the "King
Eddie"; guests gush over the "flawless service", but some sniff this
"vintage" property (just over 100 years old) is getting "a little dowdy."

Metropolitan Hotel ✗ 🏋 🌊 | 19 | 20 | 19 | 17 | $149 |

Downtown Core | 108 Chestnut St. | 416-977-5000 | fax 977-9513 |
www.metropolitan.com | 362 rooms, 60 suites
The "free morning limousine service will make co-workers jealous" advise road warriors who appreciate this "boutique"-style Downtown Core
business hotel with a Cantonese restaurant, Lai Wah Heen ("go for the
dim sum"); still, the "minimalist decor" means "microscopic rooms."

Park Hyatt 🅿 🏋 ⑤ | 24 | 24 | 21 | 23 | $560 |

Bloor Yorkville | 4 Avenue Rd. | 416-925-1234 | fax 924-4933 |
800-223-1234 | www.parkhyatttoronto.com | 301 rooms, 45 suites
"To work or play" in Toronto's "chic" Yorkville area, reviewers recommend this "well-located and well-run property", a "classy", "modern"

	ROOMS	SERVICE	DINING	FACIL.	COST

hotel "in the heart of the city"; the "know-your-name service" makes this an "oasis" "for business travelers", and you can't beat the "spacious rooms" or the "great views" from the "terrific rooftop bar"; P.S. "be sure to book a massage" at the "fabulous spa."

SoHo Metropolitan Hotel ✕

| 27 | 22 | 22 | 23 | $385 |

Downtown Core | 318 Wellington St. W. | 416-599-8800 | fax 599-8801 | 866-764-6638 | www.metropolitan.com | 75 rooms, 17 suites

The "beautiful", "modern" rooms are the standout feature of this Downtown Core "avant-garde" boutique hotel that's not one bit short on "style – or expense"; enjoy "cosy down duvets, remote-control curtains", Frette linens, floor-to-ceiling windows that open and "stunning bathrooms" with German-crafted Dornbracht fixtures, "incredible" Molton Brown amenities and "heated floors"; the location is equally "great", near "many hip restaurants on King Street" and "shopping on Queen Street", and the "friendly" service and "memorable" dining at Senses also score points.

Westin Harbour Castle 🚸🏋🛏⑤🏊🍴

| 21 | 19 | 17 | 21 | $289 |

Harbourfront | 1 Harbour Sq. | 416-869-1600 | fax 869-0573 | 800-937-8461 | www.westin.com | 970 rooms, 7 suites

"Always request a harbour view" at this "big conference" favourite where the "breathtaking" vistas of Lake Ontario make stays "worth every penny"; "renovated rooms breathe new life" into "previously dated decor" with "flat-screen TVs, great bathrooms", top-notch amenities and that famous 'Heavenly bed'; while fans find that the "terrific staff" goes "beyond the basics", naysayers caution that "service is uneven" and the "revolving restaurant is for tourists only."

Windsor Arms ⑪⑤🏊

| 23 | 23 | 22 | 21 | $331 |

Bloor Yorkville | 18 St. Thomas St. | 416-971-9666 | fax 921-9121 | 800-525-4800 | www.windsorarmshotel.com | 2 rooms, 26 suites

"Celebrities who want to stay unnoticed" hide out at this 1927 landmark turned "elegant" boutique hotel, an "intimate" property that's full of "thoughtful amenities" (like "fluffy comforters" and a "lovely spa"); the Bloor Yorkville location is prime for "upscale shopping", and you can revive yourself afterwards with "scrumptious high tea" in the "spectacular dining room"; if a few critics cry "pretentious", supporters say it "gets our vote."

INDEXES

Cuisines

Includes restaurant names, neighbourhoods and Food ratings. 🔏 indicates places with the highest ratings, popularity and importance.

AMERICAN (NEW)

Boba | **Bloor Yorkville**	26
Brassaii | **King W**	20
Edward Levesque's | **Leslieville**	-‿
🔏 Jump Café | **Financial Dist**	21

ASIAN FUSION

🔏 Lee | **King W**	27
Monsoon | **Entertainment Dist**	21
Supermarket | **Chinatown/ Kensington**	21
🔏 Susur | **King W**	27

BARBECUE

Phil's Original BBQ | **Little Italy**	22

BRAZILIAN

Cajú | **Queen W Gallery Dist**	-‿

BRITISH

Chippy's | **multi. loc.**	23

CANADIAN

🔏 Canoe | **Financial Dist**	26
Gallery Grill | **S Annex**	24
🔏 George | **Downtown Core**	26
Inn on the Twenty | **Jordan**	23
NEW Jamie Kennedy/ Gardiner | **Bloor Yorkville**	-‿
🔏 Jamie Kennedy | **St. Lawrence**	25
Trapper's | **N Toronto**	20

NEW trevor | **Downtown Core**	-‿
Vineland Estates | **Vineland**	26

CHINESE

(* dim sum specialist)

Asian Legend | **multi. loc.**	19
Dragon Dynasty* | **Scarborough**	20
EAST! Asian* | **Queen W**	17
House of Chan | **Forest Hill**	21
NEW Lai Toh Heen* | **Midtown**	-‿
🔏 Lai Wah Heen* | **Downtown Core**	27
Lee Garden | **Chinatown/ Kensington**	23
Pearl Harbourfront* | **Harbourfront**	21
Peter's Chung King | **Chinatown/Kensington**	21
Pink Pearl* | **Bloor Yorkville**	19
Swatow | **Chinatown/ Kensington**	21

COFFEE SHOPS/DINERS

Aunties & Uncles | **S Annex**	22

CONTINENTAL

Across The Road | **Midtown**	22
Bloom | **Bloor W Vill**	24
🔏 Bymark | **Financial Dist**	25
Byzantium | **Church/Wellesley**	19
Far Niente | **Financial Dist**	-‿
Lakes | **Rosedale/Summerhill**	20
🔏 North 44° | **N Toronto**	27

Opus | **Annex**	26
Pangaea | **Bloor Yorkville**	25
Peller Estates | **Niagara/Lake**	26
Z Scaramouche | **Forest Hill**	28
Trapper's | **N Toronto**	20

DELIS

Moe Pancer's | **Downsview**	22

ECLECTIC

Annona | **Bloor Yorkville**	20
Avenue | **Bloor Yorkville**	22
Brownes | **Rosedale/ Summerhill**	19
Centro | **N Toronto**	24
NEW Colborne Lane | **Downtown Core**	⌐
Courtyard Café | **Bloor Yorkville**	⌐
Flow | **Bloor Yorkville**	17
NEW Fuzion | **Downtown Core**	⌐
NEW Globe Bistro | **Danforth/ Greektown**	⌐
Hemispheres | **Downtown Core**	23
Kalendar | **Little Italy**	⌐
NEW Kultura | **Downtown Core**	⌐
Lobby | **Bloor Yorkville**	19
Pangaea | **Bloor Yorkville**	25
Senses | **Entertainment Dist**	24
NEW Spice Room | **Bloor Yorkville**	⌐
Swan | **Queen W Gallery Dist**	24
Terra | **Thornhill**	25
Tomi-Kro | **Leslieville**	21
Universal Grill | **Hillcrest/ Davenport**	20

EUROPEAN (MODERN)

Corner House | **Annex**	24
NEW Mirabelle | **Midtown**	⌐

FRENCH

Avant Goût | **Rosedale/ Summerhill**	⌐
Batifole | **Riverdale**	25
Z Bistro 990 | **Downtown Core**	23
Bonjour Brioche | **Leslieville**	23
Didier | **Midtown**	22
Eigensinn Farm | **Singhampton**	29
Epic | **Financial Dist**	24
Jacques' Bistro | **Bloor Yorkville**	22
Z Jamie Kennedy | **St. Lawrence**	25
Lakes | **Rosedale/Summerhill**	20
Le Trou Normand | **Bloor Yorkville**	20
Marcel's | **Entertainment Dist**	20
Mildred Pierce | **King W**	25
NEW Opal Jazz | **Queen W W**	⌐
Z Perigee | **Distillery Dist**	27
Sultan's Tent | **St. Lawrence**	20
Z Susur | **King W**	27

FRENCH (BISTRO)

beerbistro | **Financial Dist**	18
Biff's Bistro | **St. Lawrence**	21
Z Bistro/Bakery Thuet | **King W**	27
Bodega | **Grange Pk**	22
Crush Wine Bar | **King W**	22
Fat Cat Bistro | **Forest Hill**	25
Gamelle | **Little Italy**	22
Holt Renfrew | **Bloor Yorkville**	20

La Palette | **Chinatown/ Kensington** — 23

Le Paradis | **Annex** — 21

Le Sélect | **Entertainment Dist** — 21

Matignon | **Downtown Core** — 22

Merlot | **Islington/Kingsway** — 20

Pony | **Little Italy** — 18

Provence Délices | **Cabbagetown** — –

Rosebud, The | **Queen W W** — –

Savoy | **Downtown Core** — 17

Smalltalk Bakery | **Leaside** — 23

FRENCH (NEW)

Amuse-Bouche | **King W** — 23

☑ Auberge Pommier | **York Mills** — 24

☑ Célestin | **Midtown** — 27

Czehoski | **Queen W W** — 19

Fat Cat Bistro | **Forest Hill** — 25

Herbs | **N Toronto** — 22

JOV | **Leaside** — 25

Messis | **S Annex** — 23

Smalltalk Bakery | **Leaside** — 23

☑ Truffles | **Bloor Yorkville** — 26

GREEK

Pan on Danforth | **Danforth/ Greektown** — 19

INDIAN

Babur | **Queen W** — 22

Cuisine of India | **Willowdale** — 22

Host | **multi. loc.** — 23

Indian Rice Factory | **Annex** — 21

Natarãj | **Annex** — 20

Sher E Punjab | **Danforth/ Greektown** — 23

Xacutti | **Little Italy** — 25

IRISH

Allen's | **Danforth/Greektown** — 19

ITALIAN

(N=Northern; S=Southern)

Across The Road | N | **Midtown** — 22

NEW Balsam | **The Beach** — –

bar_one | **Queen W Gallery Dist** — 19

Bellini's | N | **Bloor Yorkville** — 21

Biagio | N | **St. Lawrence** — 20

College St. Bar | **Little Italy** — 19

Coppi | N | **N Toronto** — 21

NEW Cucina | S | **Little Italy** — –

Czehoski | **Queen W W** — 19

Ferro | S | **Hillcrest/Davenport** — 21

Five Doors North | S | **Midtown** — 20

Fusilli | S | **Corktown** — 21

Gio Rana's | **Leslieville** — 23

grano | **Midtown** — 19

Grappa | **Little Italy** — 20

☑ Il Fornello | **multi. loc.** — 18

Il Mulino | **Forest Hill** — 26

Il Posto | **Bloor Yorkville** — 21

La Bruschetta | N | **Corso Italia** — 22

La Fenice | **Entertainment Dist** — 21

Mistura | **Annex** — 25

MoDo | **Bloor Yorkville** — –

Positano | **Midtown** — 22

Prego Della Piazza | **Bloor Yorkville** — 19

☑ Scaramouche Pasta Bar | **Forest Hill** — 27

7 Numbers	S	**Danforth/ Greektown**	23
NEW Sopra Upper Lounge	**Bloor Yorkville**	–
Sotto	**multi. loc.**	23
Studio Cafe	**Bloor Yorkville**	22
Z Terroni	S	**multi. loc.**	22
Toulà	N	**Harbourfront**	16
Tratt. Fieramosca	S	**Annex**	19
Tratt. Giancarlo	N	**Little Italy**	24
Tutti Matti	N	**Entertainment Dist**	22
Vertical	S	**Financial Dist**	–
Zucca Trattoria	**Midtown**	24

JAPANESE

(* sushi specialist)

Blowfish*	**King W**	25
NEW Doku 15*	**Downtown Core**	–
EDO*	**Forest Hill**	24
EDO-ko*	**Forest Hill**	23
Fune	**Entertainment Dist**	20
Z Hiro Sushi*	**St. Lawrence**	27
Izakaya	**St. Lawrence**	19
NEW kaiseki-SAKURA	**Downtown Core**	–
Katsura	**Don Mills**	22
Ki*	**Financial Dist**	21
Nami*	**St. Lawrence**	24
Z Sushi Kaji*	**Mimico**	29
Sushi on Bloor*	**Annex**	20

KOREAN

Korea House	**Koreatown**	21

MEDITERRANEAN

Z Auberge Pommier	**York Mills**	24
Z Bistro 990	**Downtown Core**	23

Crush Wine Bar	**King W**	22
Z Lee	**King W**	27
NEW Leslie Jones	**Leslieville**	–
Lolita's Lust	**Danforth/ Greektown**	21
Millie's Bistro	**N Toronto**	22
Z Oro	**Downtown Core**	27
Z Perigee	**Distillery Dist**	27
NEW Quince	**Midtown**	–
Z Splendido	**S Annex**	27
Studio Cafe	**Bloor Yorkville**	22

MEXICAN

Burrito Boyz	**Entertainment Dist**	23
NEW Milagro	**Downtown Core**	–

MIDDLE EASTERN

Jerusalem	**multi. loc.**	20
Tabülè	**Midtown**	25

MOROCCAN

Boujadi	**Forest Hill**	23
Sultan's Tent	**St. Lawrence**	20

PAN-ASIAN

EAST! Asian	**Queen W**	17
Rain	**Entertainment Dist**	24
Z Spring Rolls	**multi. loc.**	19

PERUVIAN

Boulevard Café	**S Annex**	21

PIZZA

bar_one	**Queen W Gallery Dist**	19
Ferro	**Hillcrest/Davenport**	21
Z Il Fornello	**multi. loc.**	18
Z Terroni	**multi. loc.**	22

PORTUGUESE

Adega | **Downtown Core** `23`

Z Chiado/Antonio | **Little Italy** `28`

PUB FOOD

Allen's | **Danforth/Greektown** `19`

SANDWICHES

Moe Pancer's Deli | **Downsview** `22`

SEAFOOD

Adega | **Downtown Core** `23`

Cfood | **Midtown** `-`

Z Chiado/Antonio | **Little Italy** `28`

Chippy's | **Queen W** `23`

EDO | **Forest Hill** `24`

EDO-ko | **Forest Hill** `23`

House of Chan | **Forest Hill** `21`

Joso's | **Annex** `24`

Miller Tavern | **York Mills** `18`

Nami | **St. Lawrence** `24`

Oyster Boy | **Queen W Gallery Dist** `23`

Penrose Fish & Chips | **Midtown** `25`

Rodney's Oyster | **King W** `24`

Starfish Oyster Bed | **St. Lawrence** `26`

Tom Jones Steak | **St. Lawrence** `21`

Zee Grill | **Midtown** `23`

SMALL PLATES

(See also Spanish tapas specialist)

NEW Balsam | Italian | **The Beach** `-`

Z Chiado/Antonio | Portuguese | **Little Italy** `28`

NEW Doku 15 | Jap. | **Downtown Core** `-`

EAST! Asian | Pan-Asian | **Queen W** `17`

Five Doors North | Italian | **Midtown** `20`

Z George | Canadian | **Downtown Core** `26`

Gio Rana's | Italian | **Leslieville** `23`

Z Jamie Kennedy | Canadian | **St. Lawrence** `25`

NEW kaiseki-SAKURA | Jap. | **Downtown Core** `-`

Z Lee | Asian/Med | **King W** `27`

Lobby | Eclectic | **Bloor Yorkville** `19`

MoDo | Italian | **Bloor Yorkville** `-`

Rain | Pan-Asian | **Entertainment Dist** `24`

7 Numbers | Italian | **Danforth/Greektown** `23`

Supermarket | Asian Fusion | **Chinatown/Kensington** `21`

Terra | Eclectic | **Thornhill** `25`

SPANISH

(* tapas specialist)

Casa Barcelona! | **Islington/Kingsway** `21`

NEW Cava* | **Midtown** `-`

NEW Coca* | **Queen W W** `-`

NEW Torito* | **Chinatown/Kensington** `-`

STEAKHOUSES

Barberian's Steak | **Downtown Core** `23`

Fifth Grill | **Entertainment Dist** `-`

Z Harbour Sixty | **Harbourfront** `25`

House of Chan | **Forest Hill** `21`

Hy's Steak | **Financial Dist** `22`

NEW MEATing | **Midtown** `-`

Morton's Steak | **Bloor Yorkville** 23

☑ Ruth's Chris | **Downtown Core** 23

Tom Jones Steak | **St. Lawrence** 21

Tulip | **Leslieville** 19

THAI

Salad King | **Downtown Core** 25

VEGETARIAN

(* vegan)

Fresh | **multi. loc.** 20

Fressen* | **Queen W** 20

Millie's Bistro | **N Toronto** 22

VIETNAMESE

Pho Hung | **multi. loc.** 20

Restaurant Locations

Includes restaurant names, cuisines and Food ratings. **Z** indicates places with the highest ratings, popularity and importance.

Toronto

ANNEX

Chippy's | *British*	23
Corner House | *Euro.*	24
Fresh | *Veg.*	20
Host | *Indian*	23
Indian Rice Factory | *Indian*	21
Joso's | *Seafood*	24
Le Paradis | *French*	21
Mistura | *Italian*	25
Natarāj | *Indian*	20
Opus | *Continental*	26
Pho Hung | *Viet.*	20
Sushi on Bloor | *Jap.*	20
Tratt. Fieramosca | *Italian*	19

BAYVIEW VILLAGE

Asian Legend | *Chinese*	19
Z Il Fornello | *Italian/Pizza*	18
Jerusalem | *Mideast.*	20

BLOOR WEST VILLAGE

Bloom | *Continental*	24

BLOOR YORKVILLE

Annona | *Eclectic*	20
Avenue | *Eclectic*	22
Bellini's | *Italian*	21
Boba | *Amer.*	26
Courtyard Café | *Eclectic*	-
Flow | *Eclectic*	17
Holt Renfrew | *French*	20

Il Posto | *Italian*	21
Jacques' Bistro | *French*	22
NEW Jamie Kennedy/ Gardiner | *Canadian*	-
Le Trou Normand | *French*	20
Lobby | *Eclectic*	19
MoDo | *Italian*	-
Morton's Steak | *Steak*	23
Pangaea | *Continental/Eclectic*	25
Pink Pearl | *Chinese*	19
Prego Della Piazza | *Italian*	19
NEW Sopra Upper Lounge | *Italian*	-
Sotto | *Italian*	23
NEW Spice Room | *Eclectic*	-
Studio Cafe | *Italian/Med.*	22
Z Truffles | *French*	26

CABBAGETOWN

Provence Délices | *Belgian/ French*	-

CHINATOWN-KENSINGTON

Asian Legend | *Chinese*	19
La Palette | *French*	23
Lee Garden | *Chinese*	23
Peter's Chung King | *Chinese*	21
Pho Hung | *Viet.*	20
Supermarket | *Asian Fusion*	21
Swatow | *Chinese*	21
NEW Torito | *Spanish*	-

CHURCH & WELLESLEY

Byzantium | *Continental* 19

☑ Il Fornello | *Italian/Pizza* 18

CORKTOWN

Fusilli | *Italian* 21

CORSO ITALIA

La Bruschetta | *Italian* 22

DANFORTH-GREEKTOWN

Allen's | *Pub Food* 19

NEW Globe Bistro | *Eclectic* –

☑ Il Fornello | *Italian/Pizza* 18

Lolita's Lust | *Med.* 21

Pan on Danforth | *Greek* 19

7 Numbers | *Italian* 23

Sher E Punjab | *Indian* 23

DISTILLERY DISTRICT

☑ Perigee | *French/Med.* 27

DON MILLS

Katsura | *Jap.* 22

DOWNSVIEW

Moe Pancer's Deli | *Deli* 22

DOWNTOWN CORE

Adega | *Portug./Seafood* 23

Barberian's Steak | *Steak* 23

☑ Bistro 990 | *French/Med.* 23

NEW Colborne Lane | *Eclectic* –

NEW Doku 15 | *Jap.* –

NEW Fuzion | *Eclectic* –

☑ George | *Canadian* 26

Hemispheres | *Eclectic* 23

NEW kaiseki-SAKURA | *Jap.* –

NEW Kultura | *Eclectic* –

☑ Lai Wah Heen | *Chinese* 27

Matignon | *French* 22

NEW Milagro | *Mex.* –

☑ Oro | *Med.* 27

☑ Ruth's Chris | *Steak* 23

Salad King | *Thai* 25

Savoy | *French* 17

☑ Spring Rolls | *Pan-Asian* 19

☑ Terroni | *Italian/Pizza* 22

NEW trevor | *Canadian* –

ENTERTAINMENT DISTRICT

Burrito Boyz | *Mex.* 23

Fifth Grill | *Steak* –

Fune | *Jap.* 20

☑ Il Fornello | *Italian/Pizza* 18

La Fenice | *Italian* 21

Le Sélect Bistro | *French* 21

Marcel's | *French* 20

Monsoon | *Asian Fusion* 21

Rain | *Pan-Asian* 24

Senses Bakery | *Eclectic* 24

Tutti Matti | *Italian* 22

FINANCIAL DISTRICT

beerbistro | *French* 18

☑ Bymark | *Continental* 25

☑ Canoe | *Canadian* 26

Epic | *French* 24

Far Niente | *Continental* –

Hy's Steak | *Steak* 22

☑ Jump Café | *Amer.* 21

Ki | *Jap.* 21

Vertical | *Italian* –

RESTAURANTS

LOCATIONS

FOREST HILL

Boujadi	*Moroccan*	23
EDO	*Jap.*	24
EDO-ko	*Jap./Seafood*	23
Fat Cat Bistro	*French*	25
House of Chan	*Chinese/Steak*	21
Il Mulino	*Italian*	26
Jerusalem	*Mideast.*	20
⚡ Scaramouche	*Continental*	28
⚡ Scaramouche Pasta Bar	*Italian*	27
Sotto	*Italian*	23

GRANGE PARK

Bodega	*French*	22

HARBOURFRONT

⚡ Harbour Sixty	*Steak*	25
⚡ Il Fornello	*Italian/Pizza*	18
Pearl Harbourfront	*Chinese*	21
Toulà	*Italian*	16

HILLCREST-DAVENPORT

Ferro	*Italian/Pizza*	21
Universal Grill	*Eclectic*	20

ISLINGTON-KINGSWAY

Casa Barcelona!	*Spanish*	21
Merlot	*French*	20

KING WEST

Amuse-Bouche	*French*	23
⚡ Bistro/Bakery Thuet	*French*	27
Blowfish	*Jap.*	25
Brassaii	*Amer.*	20
Crush Wine Bar	*French/Med.*	22
⚡ Lee	*Asian Fusion/Med.*	27
Mildred Pierce	*French*	25

Rodney's Oyster	*Seafood*	24
⚡ Susur	*Asian Fusion/French*	27

KOREATOWN

Korea House	*Korean*	21

LEASIDE

JOV	*French*	25
Smalltalk Bakery	*French*	23

LESLIEVILLE

Bonjour Brioche	*French*	23
Edward Levesque's	*American*	–
Gio Rana's	*Italian*	23
NEW Leslie Jones	*Med.*	–
Tomi-Kro	*Eclectic*	21
Tulip	*Steak*	19

LITTLE ITALY

⚡ Chiado/Antonio	*Portug./Seafood*	28
College St. Bar	*Italian*	19
NEW Cucina	*Italian*	–
Gamelle	*French*	22
Grappa	*Italian*	20
Kalendar	*Eclectic*	–
Mini-Market	*Asian Fusion*	21
Phil's Original BBQ	*BBQ*	22
Pony	*French*	18
Tratt. Giancarlo	*Italian*	24
Xacutti	*Indian*	25

MIDTOWN

Across The Road	*Continental/Italian*	22
NEW Cava	*Spanish*	–
⚡ Célestin	*French*	27
Cfood	*Seafood*	–

Didier | *French* 22
Five Doors North | *Italian* 20
grano | *Italian* 19
🄩 Il Fornello | *Italian/Pizza* 18
NEW Lai Toh Heen | *Chinese* -
NEW MEATing | *Steak* -
NEW Mirabelle | *European* -
Penrose Fish & Chips | *Seafood* 25
Positano | *Italian* 22
NEW Quince | *Med.* -
Tabùlè | *Mideast.* 25
🄩 Terroni | *Italian/Pizza* 22
Zee Grill | *Seafood* 23
Zucca Trattoria | *Italian* 24

MIMICO

🄩 Sushi Kaji | *Jap.* 29

MISSISSAUGA

Host | *Indian* 23

NORTH TORONTO

Centro | *Eclectic* 24
Coppi | *Italian* 21
Herbs | *French* 22
Millie's Bistro | *Med.* 22
🄩 North 44° | *Continental* 27
🄩 Spring Rolls | *Pan-Asian* 19
Trapper's | *Canadian/* 20
    Continental

OAKVILLE

🄩 Il Fornello | *Italian/Pizza* 18

QUEEN WEST

Babur | *Indian* 22
Chippy's | *British* 23
EAST! Asian | *Pan-Asian* 17

Fresh | *Veg.* 20
Fressen | *Veg.* 20

QUEEN WEST GALLERY DISTRICT

bar_one | *Italian/Pizza* 19
Cajú | *Brazilian* -
Fresh | *Veg.* 20
Oyster Boy | *Seafood* 23
Swan | *Eclectic* 24

QUEEN WEST WEST

NEW Coca | *Spanish* -
Czehoski | *French/Italian* 19
NEW Opal Jazz | *French* -
Rosebud, The | *French* -
🄩 Terroni | *Italian/Pizza* 22

RICHMOND HILL

Host | *Indian* 23
🄩 Il Fornello | *Italian/Pizza* 18

RIVERDALE

Batifole | *French* 25

ROSEDALE-SUMMERHILL

Avant Goût | *French* -
Brownes Bistro | *Eclectic* 19
Lakes | *Continental/French* 20

SCARBOROUGH

Dragon Dynasty | *Chinese* 20

SOUTH ANNEX

Aunties & Uncles | *Diner* 22
Boulevard Café | *Peruvian* 21
Gallery Grill | *Canadian* 24
Messis | *French* 23
🄩 Splendido | *Med.* 27

ST. LAWRENCE

Biagio | *Italian*	20
Biff's Bistro | *French*	21
☑ Hiro Sushi | *Jap.*	27
Izakaya | *Jap.*	19
☑ Jamie Kennedy | *Canadian/ French*	25
Nami | *Jap.*	24
☑ Spring Rolls | *Pan-Asian*	19
Starfish Oyster Bed | *Seafood*	26
Sultan's Tent | *French/Moroccan*	20
Tom Jones Steak | *Steak*	21

THE BEACH

NEW Balsam | *Italian*	-
☑ Il Fornello | *Italian/Pizza*	18

THORNHILL

Asian Legend | *Chinese*	19
Terra | *Eclectic*	25

WILLOWDALE

Cuisine of India | *Indian*	22

YORK MILLS

Asian Legend | *Chinese*	19
☑ Auberge Pommier | *French/ Med.*	24
Miller Tavern | *Seafood*	18

Outlying Areas

JORDAN

Inn on the Twenty | *Canadian*	23

NIAGARA-ON-THE-LAKE

Peller Estates | *Continental*	26

SINGHAMPTON

Eigensinn Farm | *French*	29

VINELAND

Vineland Estates | *Canadian*	26

Nightlife Locations

Includes venue names and Appeal ratings. ☑ indicates places with the highest ratings, popularity and importance.

BLOOR YORKVILLE

☑ Panorama	23
☑ Roof Lounge	24

CHURCH & WELLESLEY

☑ Woody's/Sailor	23

DOWNTOWN CORE

Guvernment/Kool Haus	-

ENTERTAINMENT DISTRICT

C Lounge	20
Fluid	-
N'Awlins	20
Republik	21
☑ Second City	24
☑ Yuk Yuks	21

KING WEST

Brant House	22
Century Room	20
Wheat Sheaf	16

LITTLE ITALY

Andy Poolhall	21
El Convento Rico	-
Revival	22

PORT OF TORONTO

Docks	17

QUEEN WEST

Black Bull Hotel	17
Bovine Sex Club	18
Horseshoe Tavern	21
Rivoli Pool Hall	18
☑ Ultra Supper Club	24

QUEEN WEST GALLERY DISTRICT

☑ Drake, The	23
Social, The	22

ST. LAWRENCE

NEW Live@Courthouse	-
Rosewater Club	20

Hotel Locations

Includes hotel names and Room ratings.

BLOOR YORKVILLE

Four Seasons	24
Park Hyatt	24
Windsor Arms	23

DOWNTOWN CORE

Cosmopolitan Hotel & Spa	-
Hôtel Le Germain	-
Metropolitan	19
SoHo Metropolitan	27

FINANCIAL DISTRICT

Fairmont Royal York	19

HARBOURFRONT

Westin Harbour Castle	21

ST. LAWRENCE

Le Royal Méridien	21